Building a Multiview Inspection System with Raspberry Pi

Author: Dai Tran

Table of Contents

Introduction

The Evolution of Quality Control Systems

Quality control has long been a cornerstone of manufacturing and industrial processes. In an era where precision and efficiency drive success, the methods used for part inspection must keep pace with technological advancements. Traditionally, part inspection relied heavily on manual evaluation, where operators assessed products visually or used simple measurement tools. While effective to some extent, manual inspection is fraught with challenges: human error, inconsistency, and inefficiency.

Over the past two decades, automation has revolutionized quality control. From basic conveyor-belt scanners to sophisticated robotics, technology has enabled faster and more accurate inspections. However, these solutions often come with high costs and complex implementation processes, making them inaccessible to small and medium-sized enterprises (SMEs). The need for a cost-effective yet powerful solution is more critical than ever—and this is where your Multiview AI Part Inspection System steps in.

Inspiration Behind the System

The idea for building a Multiview AI Part Inspection System emerged from observing the gaps in existing quality control processes. As the manufacturing landscape becomes increasingly globalized, factories face diverse challenges:

1. **Time Constraints:** Rapid production cycles leave little room for thorough inspections.

2. **Diversity of Products:** With parts varying in size, shape, and material, a one-size-fits-all solution is impractical.

3.   **Resource Limitations:** SMEs often operate with tight budgets and limited access to advanced technology.

By leveraging Raspberry Pi—a powerful yet affordable computing platform—and integrating AI-driven classification, this system addresses these challenges head-on. It is designed to democratize automated quality control, making it accessible to manufacturers of all scales.

Goals of the Project

The Multiview AI Part Inspection System is built with the following objectives in mind:

1.   **Precision:** Achieve accurate detection and classification of defects, minimizing false positives and negatives.

2.   **Speed:** Implement real-time processing to keep up with rapid production lines.

3.   **Affordability:** Utilize low-cost hardware without compromising performance.

4.   **Scalability:** Design a system that can adapt to different product types and inspection needs.

5.   **User-Friendly:** Build an intuitive interface with multilingual support for global deployment.

These goals align with the vision of empowering manufacturers to maintain high-quality standards while optimizing resources.

Scope of the Book

This book is your complete guide to building the Multiview AI Part Inspection System. Whether you're an engineer, developer, or hobbyist, each chapter provides step-by-step instructions, technical insights, and practical tips to help you navigate the project. The table of contents reflects the progression from concept to execution, covering hardware setup, software development, AI training, and real-world optimization.

Each chapter is designed to stand alone, allowing readers to focus on specific aspects of the system. For instance, if you're primarily interested in the AI model, Chapter 9 dives deep into training and classification techniques. Conversely, if your focus is hardware integration, Chapters 3 through 6 offer comprehensive guidance on configuring Raspberry Pi and peripherals.

Why Raspberry Pi?

Raspberry Pi is the backbone of the system for several reasons:

1. **Affordability:** As a low-cost microcomputer, Raspberry Pi makes advanced technology accessible.

2. **Versatility:** Its GPIO pins and USB ports allow seamless integration with cameras, lights, and other peripherals.

3. **Portability:** Compact and lightweight, Raspberry Pi fits effortlessly into industrial setups.

4. **Community Support:** A thriving community provides abundant resources, tutorials, and libraries to aid development.

The decision to use Raspberry Pi underscores the book's emphasis on creating a system that balances cost and functionality.

Core Components of the System

At its core, the Multiview AI Part Inspection System consists of three pillars:

1. **Hardware:** Includes Raspberry Pi boards, high-resolution cameras, lights, speakers, and buttons.

2. **Software:** Features Python-based scripts for image processing, classification, and user interface design.

3. **AI Model:** A convolutional neural network (CNN) trained to distinguish between good and defective parts.

These components are interconnected to deliver seamless operation, enabling manufacturers to inspect parts from multiple angles and generate real-time feedback.

The Role of AI in Quality Control

Artificial intelligence has transformed countless industries, and quality control is no exception. By training AI models to recognize patterns and anomalies in images, manufacturers can automate inspections with unprecedented accuracy. Key advantages of AI-driven quality control include:

- **Consistency:** Unlike humans, AI does not suffer from fatigue or subjective biases.

- **Adaptability:** Machine learning models improve over time as they are exposed to new data.

- **Efficiency:** AI reduces inspection time while increasing throughput.

This book empowers readers to harness the potential of AI for part inspection, paving the way for smarter and more efficient manufacturing practices.

Multiview Inspection: A Game-Changer

Traditional inspection systems often rely on single-camera setups, which can miss defects that are not visible from one angle. The Multiview AI Part Inspection System overcomes this limitation by employing four cameras to capture images from multiple perspectives. This approach offers several benefits:

1. **Comprehensive Coverage:** Ensures every side of the part is inspected.

2. **Improved Accuracy:** Reduces the likelihood of undetected defects.

3. **Versatility:** Handles parts with complex shapes or geometries.

7

By integrating multiview inspection with AI classification, the system sets a new standard for quality control.

Practical Applications

The system is designed to cater to a wide range of industries, including:

- **Automotive:** Inspecting engine components, gears, and safety-critical parts.

- **Electronics:** Checking circuit boards, connectors, and sensors for defects.

- **Pharmaceuticals:** Ensuring the integrity of packaging and medical devices.

- **Consumer Goods:** Verifying the quality of products like appliances and furniture.

The flexibility of the system makes it suitable for any scenario where part inspection is vital.

Challenges and Solutions

While the system addresses many challenges, certain hurdles may arise during development:

1. **Hardware Compatibility:** Ensuring seamless integration between Raspberry Pi and peripherals.

2. **AI Model Performance:** Achieving high accuracy with limited training data.

3. **User Accessibility:** Developing an intuitive interface for operators with varying levels of expertise.

This book provides solutions to these challenges, helping you build a system that is both functional and reliable.

A Roadmap for Success

The journey of building the Multiview AI Part Inspection System is both exciting and rewarding. As you progress through the chapters, you will acquire skills in hardware configuration, software development, AI training, and real-world optimization. Each step brings you closer to creating a system that not only meets your needs but also sets a benchmark for innovation in quality control.

Conclusion

The introduction of this book serves as a springboard for exploring the intricacies of building a Multiview AI Part Inspection System with Raspberry Pi. It highlights the motivation, goals, and potential impact of the project while providing a clear roadmap for success. As you delve into subsequent chapters, you will gain the knowledge and tools to transform a compelling concept into a tangible solution—one that revolutionizes part inspection and empowers manufacturers worldwide.

System Overview

Introduction to the System

The Multiview AI Part Inspection System marks a significant leap in automated quality control. Utilizing Raspberry Pi technology, combined with artificial intelligence and multi-camera support, the system is designed to inspect parts efficiently, accurately, and in real-time. The system aims to replace conventional manual inspection processes, which can be inconsistent and labor-intensive, with a robust, intelligent solution capable of multi-angle analysis and high-speed detection.

At its core, this system integrates hardware, software, and AI in a cohesive framework, enabling end-to-end inspection, classification, defect notification, and real-time logging. The modular architecture ensures scalability for industries of varying sizes and adaptability to different inspection use cases.

Key Objectives

The system is built to achieve several objectives:

- **Enhanced Efficiency:** Drastically reduce inspection time through real-time processing.

- **High Accuracy:** Leverage AI to minimize human error and improve defect detection rates.

- **Cost-Effectiveness:** Provide an affordable yet capable solution using Raspberry Pi boards.

- **Flexibility:** Enable multilingual support and easy customization to fit specific requirements.

- **Scalability:** Accommodate additional hardware or software modules for more complex applications.

Functional Architecture

The Multiview AI Part Inspection System comprises several interconnected modules that work harmoniously to perform tasks. These modules are:

1. **Hardware Setup:** Includes Raspberry Pi boards, cameras, GPIO peripherals like lights, speakers, and buttons.

2. **Software Framework:** Powered by Python and AI libraries, such as TensorFlow and OpenCV, for image processing and classification.

3. **AI Model:** The machine learning model is trained to distinguish between good and bad parts based on the uploaded images.

4. **Graphical User Interface (GUI):** The user-facing component, built with multilingual support, allowing intuitive operation.

5. **Real-Time Logging & Notifications:** Records all activities locally and in Google Drive, and triggers notifications for defects.

6. **Weekly Retraining:** A module for updating the AI model with fresh data for continuous improvement.

System Flow

The workflow is structured to ensure seamless interaction between different components:

1. **Image Acquisition:** Four cameras capture the part images from multiple angles.

2. **Data Processing:** Images are pre-processed for noise reduction and fed into the AI model for analysis.

3. **Classification:** The AI model categorizes parts as "Good" or "Defective."

4. **Alerts:** Defective parts trigger an audio alert system and a visual notification on the GUI.

5. **Logging:** Classification results are saved locally and synced to Google Drive.

6. **Retraining:** At regular intervals, the AI model is retrained using newly acquired images to ensure adaptability.

Hardware Overview

Raspberry Pi

Raspberry Pi is the backbone of the system, chosen for its affordability, compact form factor, and sufficient processing power for basic AI tasks. Four Raspberry Pi boards are utilized to operate four cameras, ensuring optimal image acquisition.

Cameras

High-resolution cameras provide clear and detailed images of parts. The multi-camera setup ensures 360-degree inspection capability, capturing all sides and angles to improve defect detection.

GPIO Peripherals

Additional components include:

- **Lights:** Illuminate parts for consistent image quality.

- **Speakers:** Provide audio alerts for defective parts.

- **Buttons:** Allow users to start the inspection process and reset counters.

Software Design

The software layer integrates multiple tools and libraries:

- **Python:** The programming language of choice for its extensive libraries and ease of use.

- **OpenCV:** Handles image processing, including resizing, filtering, and feature extraction.

- **TensorFlow:** Powers the AI model for classification tasks.

- **Custom GUI:** Developed for user interaction, featuring multilingual options for global deployment.

AI Model Overview

The AI model is central to the system's intelligence. It is a supervised classification model trained on labeled images of good and defective parts. By using techniques such as data augmentation, the model is equipped to handle variations in lighting, angles, and part positioning.

Benefits and Impact

This inspection system offers numerous benefits:

- **Consistent Quality:** AI ensures reliability in detecting even the smallest defects.

- **High Productivity:** Quick processing enables faster throughput without compromising accuracy.

- **User-Friendly Design:** The intuitive GUI empowers operators to use the system with minimal training.

- **Environmental Impact:** The use of Raspberry Pi aligns with sustainable practices due to its energy efficiency.

Challenges and Solutions

While the system is designed to be robust, certain challenges might arise:

1. **Hardware Compatibility:** Ensuring seamless communication between all hardware components.

   - *Solution:* Thorough testing during setup and integration phases.

2. **AI Model Accuracy:** Initial models may struggle with rare defects.

      ○   *Solution:* Incremental improvement via weekly retraining and larger datasets.

3. **Multilingual Support:** Developing a comprehensive language database for GUI and audio alerts.

      ○   *Solution:* Collaborate with linguistic experts for accurate translations.

Future Possibilities

The modular nature of the system opens doors for future improvements:

- **Advanced AI Techniques:** Incorporation of deep learning methods for even better accuracy.

- **IoT Integration:** Enabling remote monitoring and control of the system via the Internet of Things.

- **Enhanced Scalability:** Supporting more cameras and components for larger-scale inspections.

Required Hardware

Introduction

Building a robust Multiview AI Part Inspection System begins with assembling the right hardware components. This chapter outlines the essential devices and peripherals required, detailing their significance and role within the system. From the powerful Raspberry Pi boards to the precision of high-resolution cameras, every component has been carefully selected for optimal performance. The modular design ensures adaptability, scalability, and cost efficiency, making this solution accessible to users from various industries.

Core Components

1. Raspberry Pi Boards

The Raspberry Pi serves as the heart of this inspection system. Known for its versatility, affordability, and compact size, the Raspberry Pi is perfect for managing the system's computational and interfacing needs. Depending on the complexity of your inspection process, you may require multiple Raspberry Pi units to support multi-camera configurations.

Recommended Models:

- Raspberry Pi 4 Model B (4GB or 8GB RAM): Offers sufficient processing power for real-time AI inference and image processing.

- Raspberry Pi Zero 2 W: Can be used for additional peripheral integration if needed.

Key Features:

- Quad-core processor for fast computation.

- Multiple USB and GPIO ports for connecting cameras and other peripherals.

- Compact size for easy mounting in constrained environments.

2. Cameras

The success of a Multiview AI Part Inspection System depends on the quality of the images captured. High-resolution cameras are essential for detailed visual inspection, ensuring that minute defects are not overlooked. The system requires four cameras to provide a comprehensive 360-degree view of each part.

Recommended Specifications:

- 1080p resolution or higher for crisp image quality.
- Adjustable focus to cater to varying part sizes.
- Wide-angle lenses for broader coverage if parts are large.

Popular Options:

- Raspberry Pi Camera Module 3: An official camera module with excellent compatibility.
- Arducam for Raspberry Pi: Offers higher resolution and advanced features for demanding applications.

3. Lighting System

Proper illumination is crucial for capturing clear images. A well-lit environment eliminates shadows, enhances contrast, and highlights defects that might be missed in low light. The lighting system should be adjustable to cater to different materials and surfaces.

Recommendations:

- LED ring lights mounted around each camera for uniform lighting.
- Adjustable brightness controls to optimize image quality under varying conditions.

4. Speakers

The audio alert system is a key component for notifying users about defective parts in real time. Compact speakers connected via GPIO pins can deliver clear and audible notifications.

Recommended Features:

- Compact size for easy integration.

- Adequate volume for factory floor environments.

- Compatibility with Raspberry Pi GPIO outputs.

5. Buttons and Switches

Physical buttons offer a straightforward way to interact with the system. These can be used for initiating inspections, resetting counters, or toggling system states.

Suggested Buttons:

- Momentary push buttons with LED indicators to provide visual feedback.

- Waterproof and dustproof designs for industrial environments.

6. Enclosure and Mounting

An appropriate enclosure protects the hardware components from environmental factors such as dust, moisture, and accidental damage. Mounting solutions ensure stability and proper alignment of cameras and other peripherals.

Recommendations:

- Custom-built acrylic or metal enclosures with ventilation holes.

- Adjustable camera mounts for precise positioning.

Networking and Storage

1. Network Connectivity

Reliable network connectivity is essential for syncing data with cloud storage and enabling remote monitoring. The Raspberry Pi comes with built-in Wi-Fi and Ethernet options.

Additional Hardware:

- USB Wi-Fi adapters for improved signal strength.

- Ethernet cables for wired connections in industrial settings.

2. Storage Devices

Adequate storage is required for saving images, logs, and AI models. While the Raspberry Pi supports microSD cards, external storage devices can be used for larger datasets.

Storage Options:

- High-speed microSD cards (32GB or higher) for the operating system and software.

- External USB drives or SSDs for storing images and logs.

Power Supply

A stable and reliable power supply is critical for uninterrupted operation. The Raspberry Pi and its peripherals must be powered adequately to ensure consistent performance.

Recommendations:

- Official Raspberry Pi power adapters for each board.

- Surge protectors and uninterruptible power supplies (UPS) to safeguard against power fluctuations.

Assembly and Wiring

The assembly process involves connecting all components in a cohesive layout. Proper wiring and cable management are crucial for maintaining system reliability and ease of troubleshooting.

Tips:

- Use color-coded cables for easy identification.
- Secure cables with clips or zip ties to prevent accidental disconnections.

Cost Considerations

One of the primary advantages of this system is its cost-effectiveness. By leveraging Raspberry Pi and open-source components, the overall expenses are kept minimal without compromising functionality. Below is a rough cost estimate for the essential hardware:

Component	Approximate Cost (USD)
Raspberry Pi 4 Model B	$35-$75
Camera Modules (x4)	$100-$160
LED Ring Lights	$20-$50
Speakers	$10-$25
Buttons	$5-$15
Enclosure and Mounts	$30-$60
Storage Devices	$20-$50
Power Adapters and UPS	$20-$70
Total	$240-$505

Future Hardware Enhancements

The modular design of the system allows for future upgrades. Possible enhancements include:

- **High-Speed Cameras:** For inspecting rapidly moving parts.

- **Thermal Cameras:** To detect defects related to temperature irregularities.

- **Robot Integration:** For automating part handling and positioning.

Summary

This chapter provides a comprehensive guide to the hardware required for building the Multiview AI Part Inspection System. From the versatile Raspberry Pi boards to the precision of high-resolution cameras, every component plays a crucial role in ensuring the system's effectiveness. By carefully selecting and assembling the hardware, users can create a reliable, efficient, and scalable inspection solution tailored to their specific needs.

Setting Up Raspberry Pi and OS

Introduction

Setting up the Raspberry Pi forms the foundation of your Multiview AI Part Inspection System. This compact yet powerful computer serves as the processing unit, managing image capture, AI computations, and system interactions. Before diving into software installations and configurations, it's essential to properly set up your Raspberry Pi hardware and operating system.

In this chapter, we will walk you through every step required to prepare your Raspberry Pi for the tasks ahead. Whether you're a seasoned user or new to the Raspberry Pi ecosystem, this guide ensures you're equipped to move forward confidently.

4.1 Choosing the Right Raspberry Pi Model

As discussed in the previous chapter, selecting the appropriate Raspberry Pi model is crucial. For our system, we recommend:

- **Raspberry Pi 4 Model B:** Its quad-core processor and 4GB/8GB RAM ensure smooth performance for AI inference and multi-camera setups.

- **Raspberry Pi OS Compatibility:** Ensure that your Raspberry Pi model supports the latest version of Raspberry Pi OS.

Other considerations include available USB ports for camera connections and support for peripherals like buttons and GPIO-controlled lights.

4.2 Gathering the Necessary Accessories

Before beginning the setup, ensure you have the following accessories:

- MicroSD card (32GB or higher) with high read/write speeds.

21

- Official Raspberry Pi power adapter to avoid power-related issues.

- HDMI cable and monitor for initial setup and troubleshooting.

- USB keyboard and mouse.

- Optional: A cooling fan or heatsinks to manage heat during intensive operations.

4.3 Installing Raspberry Pi OS

4.3.1 Choosing the OS

We will use **Raspberry Pi OS (64-bit, Lite or Full)**, as it provides a robust platform for running Python, OpenCV, and TensorFlow.

4.3.2 Downloading the OS

1. Visit the official Raspberry Pi website and download the Raspberry Pi Imager tool.

2. Install the tool on your computer.

4.3.3 Writing the OS to the MicroSD Card

1. Insert the microSD card into your computer.

2. Launch the Raspberry Pi Imager tool and select:

   o **Operating System:** Choose "Raspberry Pi OS (64-bit)."

   o **Storage:** Select your microSD card.

3. Click "Write" and wait for the process to complete.

4.3.4 Initial Boot and Configuration

1. Insert the microSD card into the Raspberry Pi and power it on.

2. Follow the on-screen instructions to:

   o Set up your Wi-Fi connection.

- o Change the default password for security.
- o Configure your location and keyboard layout.

3. Perform a system update:

```bash
sudo apt update
sudo apt upgrade -y
```

4.4 Enabling SSH and Headless Mode

If you plan to operate the Raspberry Pi remotely (headless mode), enable SSH:

1. Create an empty file named ssh in the /boot directory of the microSD card.

2. Reinsert the card into the Raspberry Pi and boot it.

3. Use an SSH client (e.g., PuTTY) to access the Raspberry Pi:

```bash
ssh pi@<your-pi-ip-address>
```

4.5 Expanding File System and Configuring Memory

To optimize performance:

1. Expand the file system:

```bash
sudo raspi-config
```

Navigate to **Advanced Options > Expand Filesystem** and reboot.

2. Configure memory split between GPU and CPU for better AI processing:

```bash
sudo nano /boot/config.txt
```

Add or modify:

```txt
gpu_mem=256
```

4.6 Installing Basic Utilities

Install essential tools and packages:

```bash
sudo apt install -y git vim htop net-tools build-essential
```

4.7 Ensuring System Security

1. Change the default username and password to prevent unauthorized access:

```bash
sudo adduser newusername
sudo usermod -aG sudo newusername
sudo deluser pi
```

2. Set up a firewall using ufw:

24

```bash
sudo apt install ufw
sudo ufw enable
sudo ufw allow ssh
```

4.8 Configuring USB and GPIO Ports

4.8.1 USB Ports

Connect your cameras and ensure they are recognized:

```bash
lsusb
```

4.8.2 GPIO Pins

Install the GPIO library for Python:

```bash
sudo apt install python3-rpi.gpio
```

Test GPIO functionality with a simple script:

```python
import RPi.GPIO as GPIO
GPIO.setmode(GPIO.BCM)
GPIO.setup(18, GPIO.OUT)
GPIO.output(18, GPIO.HIGH)
```

4.9 Setting Up Remote Access

Enable additional remote access options, such as VNC or Samba, for file sharing and remote control:

```bash
sudo apt install realvnc-vnc-server samba
```

4.10 Creating Backups

To avoid starting from scratch in case of failure, create a backup image of your microSD card using tools like Balena Etcher or dd on Linux:

```bash
sudo dd if=/dev/sdX of=raspberry_pi_backup.img bs=4M
```

4.11 Optimizing Performance

1. Overclock the Raspberry Pi for better performance (optional):

    o Edit the /boot/config.txt file:

```txt
over_voltage=6
arm_freq=2000
gpu_freq=750
```

    o Reboot the Raspberry Pi.

2. Monitor system performance using htop or vcgencmd:

```bash
vcgencmd measure_temp
```

Challenges and Troubleshooting

Challenge: OS Installation Errors

Solution: Use verified microSD cards and reformat them with tools like SD Card Formatter.

Challenge: Overheating

Solution: Attach heatsinks or a cooling fan.

Challenge: SSH Connection Issues

Solution: Ensure SSH is enabled, and the correct IP address is used.

Summary

This chapter has walked you through setting up the Raspberry Pi hardware and operating system, creating a solid foundation for building the Multiview AI Part Inspection System. With the Raspberry Pi optimized and secure, you're now ready to proceed to the next phase: installing the dependencies that will power your system.

Installing Dependencies (Python, OpenCV, TensorFlow, etc.)

Introduction

Dependencies form the software foundation for the Multiview AI Part Inspection System. By integrating powerful libraries and frameworks such as Python, OpenCV, and TensorFlow, the system acquires the capability to process images, train AI models, and deliver real-time results. This chapter provides a step-by-step guide to installing all necessary software components, ensuring compatibility and optimal performance on Raspberry Pi.

From programming languages to machine learning tools, we'll cover the installation and configuration processes in detail. By the end of this chapter, your Raspberry Pi will be equipped with a fully functional software environment capable of handling image processing and AI tasks.

5.1 Preparing the Raspberry Pi for Software Installation

Before installing dependencies, ensure your Raspberry Pi OS is updated and ready:

1. Update system packages:

```bash
Bash                                                    Copy

sudo apt update
sudo apt upgrade -y
```

2. Install basic developer tools:

```bash
sudo apt install -y build-essential git wget curl vim
```

5.2 Installing Python

Python is the backbone of the software environment for this system due to its versatility and rich ecosystem of libraries.

5.2.1 Checking Pre-installed Python

Raspberry Pi OS typically includes Python 3. Verify the installation:

```bash
python3 --version
```

5.2.2 Installing Python 3.9 or Higher

If an updated version is needed:

1. Install prerequisites:

```bash
sudo apt install -y libffi-dev libssl-dev zlib1g-dev libbz2-dev libreadl:
```

sudo apt install -y libffi-dev libssl-dev zlib1g-dev libbz2-dev libreadline-dev libsqlite3-dev

2. Download and compile Python:

29

```bash
cd /usr/src
sudo wget https://www.python.org/ftp/python/3.9.0/Python-3.9.0.tgz
sudo tar xzf Python-3.9.0.tgz
cd Python-3.9.0
sudo ./configure --enable-optimizations
sudo make altinstall
```

3. Confirm installation:

```bash
python3.9 --version
```

5.3 Setting Up a Virtual Environment

Using a virtual environment isolates your project dependencies, avoiding conflicts:

```bash
sudo apt install -y python3-venv
python3 -m venv ai_inspection_env
source ai_inspection_env/bin/activate
```

5.4 Installing OpenCV

OpenCV is crucial for image processing tasks such as noise reduction, edge detection, and feature extraction.

5.4.1 Installing Dependencies

Install required libraries:

```bash
sudo apt install -y cmake libgtk-3-dev libcanberra-gtk3-dev libjpeg-dev libp
```

sudo apt install -y cmake libgtk-3-dev libcanberra-gtk3-dev libjpeg-dev libpng-dev libtiff-dev libavcodec-dev libavformat-dev libswscale-dev libv4l-dev

5.4.2 Installing OpenCV from Source

1. Clone the OpenCV repository:

```bash
git clone https://github.com/opencv/opencv.git
git clone https://github.com/opencv/opencv_contrib.git
cd opencv
mkdir build && cd build
```

2. Compile OpenCV:

```bash
cmake -D CMAKE_BUILD_TYPE=Release -D CMAKE_INSTALL
make -j4
sudo make install
```

cmake -D CMAKE_BUILD_TYPE=Release -D CMAKE_INSTALL_PREFIX=/usr/local -D OPENCV_EXTRA_MODULES_PATH=../../opencv_contrib/modules ..

make -j4

sudo make install

3. Test installation:

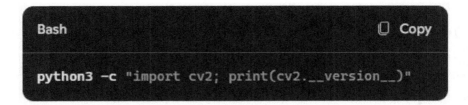

```bash
python3 -c "import cv2; print(cv2.__version__)"
```

5.5 Installing TensorFlow

TensorFlow is the machine learning framework that powers the AI model in your system.

5.5.1 Installing TensorFlow for Raspberry Pi

1. Install TensorFlow using pip:

```bash
pip install tensorflow
```

2. Verify installation:

```bash
python3 -c "import tensorflow as tf; print(tf.__ve
```

python3 -c "import tensorflow as tf; print(tf.__version__)"

5.6 Additional Libraries and Tools

Install other essential libraries:

32

```bash
pip install numpy pandas matplotlib scikit-learn
```

5.7 Managing Camera Drivers

Ensure camera compatibility by installing and configuring drivers:

1. Install v4l-utils:

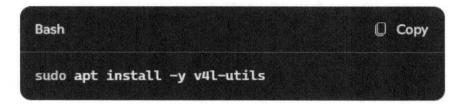

```bash
sudo apt install -y v4l-utils
```

2. Test camera connectivity:

```bash
v4l2-ctl --list-devices
```

5.8 Setting Up GPIO Control

Install the necessary library for controlling GPIO pins:

```bash
pip install RPi.GPIO
```

5.9 Ensuring System Security

To prevent unauthorized access during software installation:

33

1. Configure firewall rules:

```bash
Bash                                    Copy

sudo ufw allow ssh
sudo ufw enable
```

2. Secure the Python environment by restricting file permissions:

```bash
Bash                                    Copy

chmod -R 750 ai_inspection_env
```

Challenges and Troubleshooting

Challenge: OpenCV Installation Errors

Solution: Verify dependencies are installed correctly and rerun cmake.

Challenge: TensorFlow Compatibility

Solution: Use lightweight alternatives like TensorFlow Lite if issues arise.

Challenge: Python Version Conflicts

Solution: Use virtual environments to manage dependencies.

Summary

This chapter provides step-by-step instructions for installing dependencies critical to the operation of your Multiview AI Part Inspection System. By setting up Python, OpenCV, TensorFlow, and other libraries, your Raspberry Pi is now equipped to perform advanced image processing and AI tasks. With these components in place, you're ready to proceed to the next phase: integrating and configuring the multi-camera setup.

Connecting and Configuring 4 Cameras

Introduction

One of the core features of the Multiview AI Part Inspection System is its ability to simultaneously capture images from four different angles. This setup ensures comprehensive inspection of parts, enabling the AI system to detect defects that may not be visible with a single-camera configuration.

This chapter provides step-by-step instructions on connecting and configuring four cameras to the Raspberry Pi. By addressing hardware setups, software configurations, synchronization, and troubleshooting, you'll establish a reliable multi-camera system ready for advanced AI applications.

6.1 Understanding the Multi-Camera Setup

Why Use Four Cameras?

The use of multiple cameras ensures that every part inspected is seen from multiple perspectives:

- **Enhanced Accuracy:** Multiview imaging allows the detection of defects on all sides of a part.

- **Comprehensive Coverage:** Reduces blind spots compared to single-camera setups.

- **Versatility:** Can accommodate parts with complex geometries and varying sizes.

6.2 Choosing Suitable Cameras

Selecting appropriate cameras for your system is essential for achieving optimal image quality and performance. You can combine Raspberry Pi-compatible cameras and USB cameras based on your system requirements.

Recommended Cameras:

1. **Raspberry Pi Camera Module 3:** Provides high-quality images and integrates seamlessly with the Raspberry Pi's CSI (Camera Serial Interface) ports.

2. **USB Webcams:** Such as Logitech C920, which are reliable and high-resolution, with plug-and-play functionality.

3. **Arducam Multi-Camera Adapter:** Allows up to four Raspberry Pi cameras to connect to a single Raspberry Pi.

Features to Look For:

- Resolution: Minimum of 1080p for clear and detailed images.
- Frame Rate: At least 30 frames per second (fps) for smooth capture.
- Compatibility: Ensure drivers are supported by Raspberry Pi OS.

6.3 Hardware Setup

Connecting Raspberry Pi Cameras

1. Power off your Raspberry Pi.

2. Locate the CSI ports on the Raspberry Pi board.

3. Attach the flat ribbon cable from the Raspberry Pi Camera Module to the CSI port. Ensure the metal contacts are facing correctly.

4. If using an Arducam Multi-Camera Adapter, connect the adapter to the CSI port and attach up to four Raspberry Pi cameras.

Connecting USB Cameras

1. Plug each USB camera into an available USB port on the Raspberry Pi. If USB ports are limited, use a powered USB hub.

2. Secure all connections to prevent accidental disconnections during operation.

Managing Power Supply

Given the additional power demands:

- Use a Raspberry Pi power adapter with a 5V/3A output.

- For USB cameras, use a powered USB hub to offload power requirements.

6.4 Enabling Camera Interfaces

To activate the cameras, adjust the Raspberry Pi settings:

1. Open the configuration tool:

```
sudo raspi-config
```

2. Navigate to **Interface Options > Camera** and enable the camera interface.

3. Reboot the Raspberry Pi:

```
sudo reboot
```

6.5 Testing Camera Connections

To verify that all cameras are connected and functional:

- Check Raspberry Pi cameras:

```bash
libcamera-hello
```

This command tests the default camera module.

- Check USB cameras:

```bash
v4l2-ctl --list-devices
```

This command lists all video devices connected to the Raspberry Pi.

6.6 Configuring Multi-Camera Software

Installing Required Libraries

Ensure necessary libraries are installed for camera operation:

1. Install OpenCV for image processing:

```bash
pip install opencv-python
```

2. Install v4l-utils for managing USB cameras:

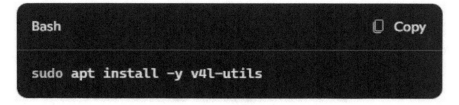

```bash
Bash                                              Copy

sudo apt install -y v4l-utils
```

Writing Python Scripts for Multi-Camera Integration

To capture images from multiple cameras, use Python scripts that combine OpenCV and threading.

Capturing from USB Cameras:

```python
Python                                            Copy

import cv2

# Initialize cameras
camera1 = cv2.VideoCapture(0)  # USB Camera 1
camera2 = cv2.VideoCapture(1)  # USB Camera 2

# Capture images
ret1, frame1 = camera1.read()
ret2, frame2 = camera2.read()

# Save images
cv2.imwrite('camera1_image.jpg', frame1)
cv2.imwrite('camera2_image.jpg', frame2)

# Release cameras
camera1.release()
camera2.release()
```

Synchronizing Multiple Cameras: To synchronize image capture, use Python threading:

40

```python
import threading
import cv2

def capture_camera(camera_index, filename):
    camera = cv2.VideoCapture(camera_index)
    ret, frame = camera.read()
    cv2.imwrite(filename, frame)
    camera.release()

# Define threads
thread1 = threading.Thread(target=capture_camera, arg
thread2 = threading.Thread(target=capture_camera, arg

# Start threads
thread1.start()
thread2.start()

# Wait for threads to complete
thread1.join()
thread2.join()
```

import threading

import cv2

def capture_camera(camera_index, filename):

    camera = cv2.VideoCapture(camera_index)

    ret, frame = camera.read()

    cv2.imwrite(filename, frame)

    camera.release()

41

```
# Define threads

thread1 = threading.Thread(target=capture_camera, args=(0,
'camera1_image.jpg'))

thread2 = threading.Thread(target=capture_camera, args=(1,
'camera2_image.jpg'))


# Start threads

thread1.start()

thread2.start()


# Wait for threads to complete

thread1.join()

thread2.join()
```

6.7 Synchronization and Testing

To ensure all cameras capture simultaneously:

1. Use timestamps to verify that captured images are aligned.

2. If synchronization issues arise:

    o Adjust software threads for better timing.

    o Use hardware triggers for precise capture.

6.8 Troubleshooting Common Issues

Issue: Cameras Not Detected

Solution:

- Check physical connections and ensure ribbon cables are securely attached.

- Verify that USB devices are recognized using lsusb.

Issue: USB Bandwidth Overload

Solution:

- Reduce camera resolution or frame rate.

- Use a USB 3.0 hub to increase bandwidth.

Issue: Image Quality Problems

Solution:

- Adjust camera settings such as exposure and white balance.

- Ensure proper lighting conditions to improve image clarity.

6.9 Optimizing Performance

Optimize the multi-camera setup for better results:

1. Reduce resolution during testing to conserve processing power.

2. Utilize OpenCV for real-time preprocessing tasks like resizing and color correction.

3. Monitor system resources using htop to avoid overload.

6.10 Future Enhancements

Hardware Upgrades

1. **High-Resolution Cameras:** Replace existing cameras with 4K models for detailed defect detection.

2. **Depth Cameras:** Incorporate depth sensors for 3D imaging.

Software Features

1. **Dynamic Camera Control:** Implement pan-tilt mechanisms for flexible positioning.

2. **Advanced Synchronization:** Use external hardware triggers for precise timing.

Summary

This chapter provides a comprehensive guide to connecting and configuring four cameras for the Multiview AI Part Inspection System. With a combination of hardware adjustments and software scripts, your system is now ready to capture synchronized multiview images. This setup lays the groundwork for training the AI model and implementing real-time defect detection in subsequent chapters.

Building the GUI for Multilingual Support

Introduction

A well-designed Graphical User Interface (GUI) is the bridge between complex system functionalities and end-users. In the context of the Multiview AI Part Inspection System, the GUI plays an integral role in providing intuitive access to the system's capabilities. It not only guides users through the inspection process but also enhances accessibility through multilingual support, empowering operators from diverse linguistic backgrounds to interact seamlessly with the system.

This chapter walks you through the process of building a custom GUI with multilingual functionality, leveraging Python and its robust frameworks. From planning the interface design to implementing real-time language switching, we will explore every aspect in detail, ensuring that your system is both user-friendly and globally applicable.

Importance of Multilingual Support

As industries continue to globalize, the workforce often comprises individuals from various linguistic regions. A GUI with multilingual capabilities ensures:

- **Inclusivity:** Operators can navigate the system in their preferred language.

- **Efficiency:** Reduced training time and errors caused by language barriers.

- **Scalability:** Broader market reach for the inspection system across different countries.

Multilingual support is more than a feature—it's a necessity for fostering adaptability and ease of use in diverse environments.

Tools and Frameworks for GUI Development

To create a robust and dynamic GUI, the following tools and frameworks are recommended:

1. **Tkinter:** A built-in Python library for creating simple and lightweight GUI applications.

2. **PyQt/PySide:** Advanced frameworks for building professional-grade GUIs with rich features.

3. **Babel Library:** A Python library for internationalization (i18n) and localization (l10n).

4. **JSON Files:** Used for storing translations in a structured and easily manageable format.

For this chapter, we will focus on using Tkinter, given its simplicity and ease of integration with Raspberry Pi.

Planning the GUI Layout

Before diving into code, it's essential to plan the layout of your GUI. The design should prioritize usability and clarity. Consider the following elements:

- **Navigation Bar:** Provides access to different sections, such as image uploads, logs, and settings.

- **Language Dropdown:** Allows users to switch between languages effortlessly.

- **Real-Time Feedback Panel:** Displays inspection results, including good and defective parts.

- **Control Buttons:** Includes options like "Start Inspection," "Reset Counter," and "Pause."

- **Status Indicators:** Shows system health, camera connectivity, and process status.

Sketching the layout on paper or using design tools like Figma can help visualize the interface before implementation.

Creating the GUI with Tkinter

Below is a step-by-step guide to building the multilingual GUI:

Step 1: Importing Libraries

Start by importing the necessary libraries:

```python
Python                                              Copy

import tkinter as tk
from tkinter import ttk
import json
```

Step 2: Setting Up Language Files

Create separate JSON files for each supported language. For example, en.json (English) and es.json (Spanish) might look like this: **en.json**:

```json
Json                                                Copy

{
    "start_button": "Start Inspection",
    "reset_button": "Reset Counter",
    "language_label": "Select Language"
}
```

es.json:

```json
{
    "start_button": "Iniciar Inspección",
    "reset_button": "Reiniciar Contador",
    "language_label": "Seleccionar Idioma"
}
```

Step 3: Loading Language Data

Write a function to load the selected language:

```python
def load_language(language_code):
    with open(f"{language_code}.json", "r") as file:
        return json.load(file)
```

Step 4: Building the Interface

Create the main GUI window and add widgets dynamically based on the
loaded language:

```python
def build_gui(language):
    root = tk.Tk()
    root.title("Multiview AI Part Inspection System")

    # Load selected language
    lang_data = load_language(language)

    # Language Dropdown
    language_label = ttk.Label(root, text=lang_data["
    language_label.pack()
    language_options = ["en", "es"]
    language_var = tk.StringVar(value="en")
    language_dropdown = ttk.Combobox(root, values=lan
    language_dropdown.pack()

    # Buttons
    start_button = ttk.Button(root, text=lang_data["s
    start_button.pack()

    reset_button = ttk.Button(root, text=lang_data["r
    reset_button.pack()

    root.mainloop()
```

def build_gui(language):

  root = tk.Tk()

  root.title("Multiview AI Part Inspection System")

  # Load selected language

  lang_data = load_language(language)

```
# Language Dropdown

language_label = ttk.Label(root, text=lang_data["language_label"])

language_label.pack()

language_options = ["en", "es"]

language_var = tk.StringVar(value="en")

language_dropdown = ttk.Combobox(root, values=language_options,
textvariable=language_var)

language_dropdown.pack()


# Buttons

start_button = ttk.Button(root, text=lang_data["start_button"])

start_button.pack()


reset_button = ttk.Button(root, text=lang_data["reset_button"])

reset_button.pack()


root.mainloop()
```

Implementing Real-Time Language Switching

To make the GUI more dynamic, allow users to switch languages without restarting the application:

1. **Event Binding:** Bind the language dropdown to a function that reloads widgets.

2. **Dynamic Update Function:**

```Python
def update_language(*args):
    new_language = language_var.get()
    lang_data = load_language(new_language)
    language_label.config(text=lang_data["language_la
    start_button.config(text=lang_data["start_button"
    reset_button.config(text=lang_data["reset_button"
```

*def update_language(*args):*

  new_language = language_var.get()

  lang_data = load_language(new_language)

  language_label.config(text=lang_data["language_label"])

  start_button.config(text=lang_data["start_button"])

  reset_button.config(text=lang_data["reset_button"])

By linking update_language to the dropdown, the GUI will reflect the new language immediately.

Enhancing the User Experience

To make the GUI more intuitive, consider the following enhancements:

- **Tooltips:** Add tooltips to buttons and fields to guide users.

- **Keyboard Shortcuts:** Allow faster navigation through keyboard inputs.

- **Responsive Design:** Ensure the interface adapts to different screen sizes, especially for touchscreen compatibility.

Testing and Optimization

Before deployment, rigorously test the GUI under different conditions:

1. **Language Coverage:** Verify translations for all supported languages.

2. **Error Handling:** Ensure the application gracefully handles missing or corrupt language files.

3. **Performance:** Test responsiveness on the Raspberry Pi to avoid delays or crashes.

Future Extensions

The multilingual GUI can be further enhanced with advanced features:

- **Voice Commands:** Enable voice control for hands-free operation.

- **Remote Access:** Allow users to interact with the GUI through a web browser or mobile app.

- **Dynamic Language Addition:** Provide a user interface for adding new languages without modifying the codebase.

Conclusion

A multilingual GUI is a cornerstone of the Multiview AI Part Inspection System, ensuring global accessibility and user satisfaction. By leveraging Python's tools and following the guidelines in this chapter, you can create an interface that is not only functional but also inclusive. As industries move toward greater automation and diversity, your system will stand out as a testament to innovation and adaptability.

Capturing and Uploading Good & Bad Part Images

Introduction

In the development of the Multiview AI Part Inspection System, the accuracy and reliability of the AI model depend significantly on the quality and diversity of the dataset used for training. This chapter focuses on the process of capturing images of parts—both "good" and "bad"—and preparing them for upload to build a robust dataset. By systematically collecting and categorizing images, you will create the foundation for training an AI model capable of precise defect detection and classification.

The Importance of High-Quality Images

Before diving into the technical aspects, it is important to recognize why image quality is crucial for AI training:

1. **Accuracy:** Clear images with minimal noise improve feature extraction during preprocessing.

2. **Diversity:** Including images of various part types, shapes, sizes, and defects ensures the AI model generalizes well.

3. **Consistency:** Uniform lighting and focus reduce variations caused by environmental factors, making the dataset more reliable.

Setting Up for Image Capture

1. Preparing the Environment

Creating a controlled environment for image capture ensures consistency and eliminates external factors that may interfere with image quality:

- **Lighting:** Use LED ring lights to illuminate the parts evenly. Avoid shadows and reflections by diffusing the light.

- **Background:** Choose a neutral background to eliminate distractions and enhance part visibility.

- **Camera Positioning:** Mount cameras securely and adjust angles for optimal coverage of the parts.

2. Camera Configuration

Configure the cameras to achieve the best possible results:

- **Resolution:** Set the camera resolution to at least 1080p for detailed images.

- **Focus:** Adjust the focus based on the size and distance of the parts.

- **Capture Settings:** Use settings like white balance and ISO to adapt to lighting conditions.

Capturing Good Part Images

Identifying "Good" Parts

Begin by selecting parts that are free of defects. These serve as the benchmark for training the AI model to recognize acceptable quality standards.

Capture Process

Follow these steps to capture images:

1. **Place the part on the inspection platform.**

2. **Capture images from multiple angles:** Use the multi-camera setup to get 360-degree coverage.

3. **Save images to labeled folders:** Organize images into folders named "Good_Parts" for easy identification.

Image Augmentation

To enhance the dataset, apply augmentation techniques to the captured images:

- **Rotation:** Simulate different part orientations.

- **Scaling:** Adjust the size to mimic variations in manufacturing processes.

- **Brightness Adjustments:** Create samples under different lighting conditions.

Capturing Bad Part Images

Identifying "Bad" Parts

Defective parts may exhibit a wide range of issues, such as cracks, misalignments, or surface abnormalities. It is important to include diverse defect types to train the model effectively.

Capture Process

Follow the same steps as for good parts but ensure defects are clearly visible:

1. **Highlight defects:** Use contrasting lighting or markers to emphasize problem areas.

2. **Capture images from multiple angles:** Defects should be visible from at least two different perspectives.

3. **Save images to labeled folders:** Organize images into folders named "Bad_Parts" with subfolders for specific defect types.

Balancing the Dataset

To avoid bias during training, ensure the number of bad part images is roughly equal to the good part images. Oversampling or augmentation can be used to achieve balance.

Uploading Images

Organizing the Dataset

Before uploading, organize the images into a structured format:

- **Root Folder:** Create a parent folder named "Dataset."

- **Subfolders:** Create subfolders for "Good_Parts" and "Bad_Parts."

- **Naming Convention:** Use descriptive filenames, such as good_part_01.jpg or bad_part_crack_01.jpg, to simplify identification.

Upload to Raspberry Pi

Transfer the images to the Raspberry Pi for preprocessing:

1. **Connect storage device:** Use an external USB drive or microSD card.

2. **Transfer files:** Copy the dataset to a designated directory on the Raspberry Pi.

Cloud Storage Integration

To ensure accessibility and backup, sync the dataset with cloud storage like Google Drive:

1. **Install Google Drive client on Raspberry Pi.**

2. **Sync folders:** Configure automatic syncing to upload new images regularly.

Preprocessing Images

Noise Reduction

Use OpenCV to remove noise from images:

```python
import cv2

def denoise_image(image_path):
    image = cv2.imread(image_path)
    denoised_image = cv2.fastNlMeansDenoisingColored(
    return denoised_image
```

import cv2

def denoise_image(image_path):

  image = cv2.imread(image_path)

  denoised_image = cv2.fastNlMeansDenoisingColored(image, None, 10, 10, 7, 21)

  return denoised_image

Image Resizing

Resize images for uniformity:

```python
def resize_image(image_path, width, height):
    image = cv2.imread(image_path)
    resized_image = cv2.resize(image, (width, height)
    return resized_image
```

def resize_image(image_path, width, height):

  image = cv2.imread(image_path)

resized_image = cv2.resize(image, (width, height))

return resized_image

Edge Detection

Highlight edges to improve defect visibility:

```python
def detect_edges(image_path):
    image = cv2.imread(image_path, cv2.IMREAD_GRAYSCA
    edges = cv2.Canny(image, threshold1=100, threshol
    return edges
```

def detect_edges(image_path):

    image = cv2.imread(image_path, cv2.IMREAD_GRAYSCALE)

    edges = cv2.Canny(image, threshold1=100, threshold2=200)

    return edges

Best Practices for Dataset Management

1. **Regular Updates:** Continuously add new images to keep the dataset relevant.

2. **Data Annotation:** Label images accurately to avoid misleading the AI model.

3. **Version Control:** Maintain different versions of the dataset for retraining purposes.

Challenges and Solutions

Challenge: Inconsistent Lighting

Solution: Use adjustable LED lights to standardize illumination.

Challenge: Limited Defective Samples

Solution: Simulate defects using image editing tools.

Challenge: File Management

Solution: Automate the organization and syncing process with scripts.

Future Considerations

As the system evolves, consider expanding the dataset to include:

1. **Additional Part Types:** Broaden the scope of inspection capabilities.

2. **Complex Defects:** Train the model to detect defects in intricate geometries.

3. **Environmental Variations:** Collect images under diverse factory conditions for greater robustness.

Conclusion

Capturing and uploading good and bad part images is the foundation for training an effective AI model. By following the guidelines in this chapter, you will build a comprehensive dataset that empowers your Multiview AI Part Inspection System to achieve high accuracy and reliability. This systematic approach not only ensures quality but also lays the groundwork for continuous improvement through regular updates and retraining.

Training the AI Model for Classification

Introduction

The AI model serves as the intelligent core of the Multiview AI Part Inspection System. By analyzing images captured by multiple cameras, it classifies parts as "Good" or "Defective" based on pre-defined criteria. This chapter outlines the process of training the AI model, from preparing the dataset to evaluating its performance, ensuring that the model is capable of high-accuracy predictions.

Effective training involves three major components: data preprocessing, model selection, and optimization. By the end of this chapter, you will have a functional AI model that serves as the backbone of your inspection system.

Understanding AI Classification

Classification is a supervised machine learning task where the model assigns labels to input data—in this case, images of parts. The success of this process depends on:

1. **Quality Dataset:** A well-balanced collection of good and defective part images.

2. **Feature Extraction:** Identifying distinguishing characteristics in images that define quality standards.

3. **Algorithm Selection:** Choosing a machine learning algorithm suitable for the given task and computational resources.

Preparing the Dataset

Before training the AI model, the dataset must be curated and preprocessed to maximize its effectiveness.

1. Data Splitting

Divide the dataset into three subsets:

- **Training Set:** 70% of images used to train the model.

- **Validation Set:** 15% of images for hyperparameter tuning and monitoring.

- **Testing Set:** 15% of images for final evaluation.

Organize images into separate folders for good and defective parts:

```
                                                    🗋 Copy

/Dataset
    /Training
        /Good_Parts
        /Bad_Parts
    /Validation
        /Good_Parts
        /Bad_Parts
    /Testing
        /Good_Parts
        /Bad_Parts
```

2. Data Augmentation

To enrich the dataset, apply augmentation techniques like rotation, flipping, and scaling using Python libraries such as TensorFlow or Keras:

```python
from tensorflow.keras.preprocessing.image import Imag

datagen = ImageDataGenerator(
    rotation_range=20,
    width_shift_range=0.2,
    height_shift_range=0.2,
    shear_range=0.2,
    zoom_range=0.2,
    horizontal_flip=True,
    fill_mode='nearest'
)

image = datagen.random_transform(image_array)
```

from tensorflow.keras.preprocessing.image import ImageDataGenerator

datagen = ImageDataGenerator(

  rotation_range=20,

  width_shift_range=0.2,

  height_shift_range=0.2,

  shear_range=0.2,

  zoom_range=0.2,

  horizontal_flip=True,

  fill_mode='nearest'

)

image = datagen.random_transform(image_array)

3. Normalization

Normalize pixel values to range between 0 and 1 to improve model efficiency:

```python
image = image / 255.0
```

Selecting the AI Model

For image classification tasks, convolutional neural networks (CNNs) are widely used due to their ability to extract spatial features. Below are options based on complexity and resources:

Option 1: Pre-trained Models

Using pre-trained models like MobileNet or ResNet speeds up development by leveraging transfer learning.

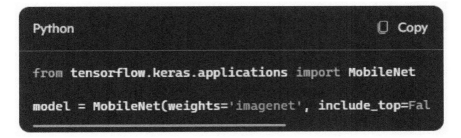

```python
from tensorflow.keras.applications import MobileNet
model = MobileNet(weights='imagenet', include_top=Fal
```

Option 2: Custom CNNs

Build a custom CNN for greater control and adaptability:

```python
from tensorflow.keras.models import Sequential
from tensorflow.keras.layers import Conv2D, MaxPoolin

model = Sequential([
    Conv2D(32, (3, 3), activation='relu', input_shape
    MaxPooling2D(pool_size=(2, 2)),
    Conv2D(64, (3, 3), activation='relu'),
    MaxPooling2D(pool_size=(2, 2)),
    Flatten(),
    Dense(128, activation='relu'),
    Dense(2, activation='softmax')
])
```

from tensorflow.keras.models import Sequential

from tensorflow.keras.layers import Conv2D, MaxPooling2D, Flatten, Dense

model = Sequential([

　　Conv2D(32, (3, 3), activation='relu', input_shape=(224, 224, 3)),

　　MaxPooling2D(pool_size=(2, 2)),

　　Conv2D(64, (3, 3), activation='relu'),

　　MaxPooling2D(pool_size=(2, 2)),

　　Flatten(),

　　Dense(128, activation='relu'),

　　Dense(2, activation='softmax')

])

Training the Model

Configuring Training Parameters

Select optimal parameters for training:

- **Batch Size:** Number of images per training iteration (e.g., 32 or 64).

- **Epochs:** Number of complete passes through the dataset (e.g., 20–50).

- **Learning Rate:** Initial rate of weight updates (e.g., 0.001).

Compiling the Model

Specify the loss function, optimizer, and evaluation metrics:

```python
model.compile(
    loss='categorical_crossentropy',
    optimizer='adam',
    metrics=['accuracy']
)
```

Training

Start training the model using the training set:

```python
history = model.fit(
    train_generator,
    epochs=20,
    validation_data=validation_generator
)
```

Evaluating Model Performance

After training, evaluate the model on the testing set to measure accuracy and loss:

```python
test_loss, test_accuracy = model.evaluate(test_genera
print("Test Accuracy:", test_accuracy)
```

test_loss, test_accuracy = model.evaluate(test_generator)

print("Test Accuracy:", test_accuracy)

Generate a confusion matrix to understand classification errors:

```python
from sklearn.metrics import confusion_matrix

cm = confusion_matrix(test_labels, predictions)
```

Fine-Tuning the Model

To improve performance, consider the following techniques:

1. **Learning Rate Scheduling:** Gradually reduce the learning rate during training.

2. **Dropout:** Prevent overfitting by randomly disabling neurons during training.

3. **Regularization:** Add penalties for large weight values to encourage simpler models.

Saving and Deploying the Model

66

Model Saving

Save the trained model for deployment:

```python
model.save('part_inspection_model.h5')
```

Loading the Model

Load the model during runtime for real-time classification:

```python
from tensorflow.keras.models import load_model

model = load_model('part_inspection_model.h5')
```

Integration with the Inspection System

Embed the trained model into the Raspberry Pi to classify images captured during inspections. Use TensorFlow Lite for optimized performance on resource-constrained devices:

```python
import tensorflow as tf

converter = tf.lite.TFLiteConverter.from_saved_model(
tflite_model = converter.convert()
```

Challenges and Solutions

Challenge: Limited Computational Power

Solution: Use transfer learning to reduce training time and computational requirements.

Challenge: Dataset Imbalance

Solution: Apply oversampling or class weighting to balance the impact of good and defective parts.

Challenge: Overfitting

Solution: Use data augmentation and regularization to enhance generalization.

Future Possibilities

To ensure continuous improvement, consider the following advancements:

1. **Advanced Architectures:** Experiment with models like EfficientNet for better accuracy.

2. **Continuous Learning:** Implement weekly retraining using newly captured images.

3. **Edge AI:** Explore hardware accelerators like Google Coral for faster inference on Raspberry Pi.

Summary

Training the AI model is a transformative process that equips your Multiview AI Part Inspection System with intelligence and precision. By following the steps outlined in this chapter, you will create a robust model capable of classifying parts with high accuracy. From dataset preparation to deployment, every aspect has been designed to ensure optimal performance and scalability, paving the way for an efficient and reliable inspection system.

Real-Time Detection with Multi-Camera Comparison

Introduction

Real-time detection is the pinnacle of automated inspection systems. By leveraging synchronized multi-camera imaging and AI-driven classification, the Multiview AI Part Inspection System provides unparalleled accuracy and efficiency in identifying defects. This chapter delves into the mechanisms of real-time detection, outlining the steps for combining multi-camera input with AI analysis, achieving synchronized defect comparison, and handling results dynamically.

Real-time capabilities are essential in modern manufacturing environments, where throughput and quality must be maintained simultaneously. By the end of this chapter, you'll have a fully operational system capable of performing real-time defect analysis and generating actionable insights.

10.1 Defining Real-Time Detection

What Is Real-Time Detection?

Real-time detection refers to the process of analyzing and responding to inputs as they occur, without noticeable delay. In the context of this system:

- Cameras capture images simultaneously from multiple angles.

- Images are fed into the AI model for classification.

- Results are displayed instantly on the GUI, with alerts for defective parts.

Benefits of Real-Time Detection

1. **Speed:** Instant feedback minimizes production delays.

2. **Accuracy:** Multi-camera input ensures comprehensive defect identification.

3. **Scalability:** Adaptable to high-speed production lines.

10.2 Architecture of the Detection System

Workflow Overview

The detection system follows these steps:

1. **Image Capture:** Cameras capture images of the part from four different angles simultaneously.

2. **Preprocessing:** Images undergo preprocessing (e.g., resizing, noise reduction) to enhance quality.

3. **AI Classification:** The trained AI model analyzes the images and categorizes parts as "Good" or "Defective."

4. **Comparison:** Results from multiple camera views are compared to confirm or reject defect classification.

5. **Output:** Final results are displayed in real time, with alerts for defective parts.

System Components

- **Hardware:** Includes Raspberry Pi boards, cameras, and GPIO peripherals (e.g., lights, speakers).

- **Software:** Python-based scripts leveraging OpenCV for image processing and TensorFlow for AI inference.

- **GUI:** Displays classification results and logs data.

10.3 Setting Up Real-Time Detection

10.3.1 Synchronizing Camera Input

Synchronization ensures that all cameras capture images at the same moment:

1. Use Python threading or multiprocessing for concurrent camera operations.

2. Implement hardware synchronization (e.g., external triggers) if higher precision is required.

Example Code for Multi-Camera Capture:

```python
import cv2
import threading

def capture_camera(camera_index, filename):
    camera = cv2.VideoCapture(camera_index)
    ret, frame = camera.read()
    cv2.imwrite(filename, frame)
    camera.release()

# Create threads for simultaneous capture
threads = []
for i in range(4):   # Assuming 4 cameras
    threads.append(threading.Thread(target=capture_ca

# Start threads
for thread in threads:
    thread.start()

# Wait for all threads to finish
for thread in threads:
    thread.join()
```

import cv2

import threading

```
def capture_camera(camera_index, filename):
    camera = cv2.VideoCapture(camera_index)
    ret, frame = camera.read()
    cv2.imwrite(filename, frame)
    camera.release()


# Create threads for simultaneous capture
threads = []
for i in range(4):  # Assuming 4 cameras
    threads.append(threading.Thread(target=capture_camera, args=(i, f'camera_{i}.jpg')))


# Start threads
for thread in threads:
    thread.start()


# Wait for all threads to finish
for thread in threads:
    thread.join()
```

10.3.2 Preprocessing Images

Preprocessing enhances image quality and reduces computational load:

- **Resizing:** Standardize dimensions for AI model input.
- **Noise Reduction:** Remove artifacts using OpenCV functions.

- **Edge Detection:** Highlight features that aid defect identification.

Preprocessing Example:

```python
def preprocess_image(image_path):
    image = cv2.imread(image_path)
    resized_image = cv2.resize(image, (224, 224))  #
    denoised_image = cv2.GaussianBlur(resized_image,
    return denoised_image
```

def preprocess_image(image_path):

  image = cv2.imread(image_path)

  resized_image = cv2.resize(image, (224, 224)) # Resize to model input dimensions

  denoised_image = cv2.GaussianBlur(resized_image, (5, 5), 0)

  return denoised_image

10.4 Integrating AI Classification

Loading the AI Model

Ensure the trained AI model is loaded and ready for inference:

```python
from tensorflow.keras.models import load_model

model = load_model('part_inspection_model.h5')
```

Running Real-Time Inference

73

1. Preprocess captured images from all cameras.

2. Feed images into the AI model for classification.

3. Aggregate results to determine the final classification.

Inference Example:

```python
def classify_image(image_path, model):
    image = preprocess_image(image_path)
    image_array = image / 255.0  # Normalize pixel va
    image_array = image_array.reshape(1, 224, 224, 3)
    prediction = model.predict(image_array)
    return prediction.argmax()  # Returns class index
```

def classify_image(image_path, model):

image = preprocess_image(image_path)

image_array = image / 255.0 # Normalize pixel values

image_array = image_array.reshape(1, 224, 224, 3) # Reshape for model input

prediction = model.predict(image_array)

return prediction.argmax() # Returns class index

Combining Results

Aggregate classifications from all cameras:

```python
results = []
for i in range(4):  # Four cameras
    result = classify_image(f'camera_{i}.jpg', model)
    results.append(result)

# Determine final classification based on majority vo
final_result = max(set(results), key=results.count)
```

results = []

for i in range(4): # Four cameras

  result = classify_image(f'camera_{i}.jpg', model)

  results.append(result)

Determine final classification based on majority vote

final_result = max(set(results), key=results.count)

10.5 Displaying Results in Real Time

GUI Integration

Update the GUI to display classification results and real-time notifications:

1. Show part status (Good/Defective) with corresponding images.

2. Trigger visual and audio alerts for defective parts.

GUI Example Code:

```python
import tkinter as tk

def update_gui(result):
    root = tk.Tk()
    root.title("Inspection Results")

    if result == 0:  # Assuming 0 = Good, 1 = Defecti
        message = "Part Status: Good"
        color = "green"
    else:
        message = "Part Status: Defective"
        color = "red"

    label = tk.Label(root, text=message, fg=color, fo
    label.pack()
    root.mainloop()

update_gui(final_result)
```

import tkinter as tk

def update_gui(result):

   root = tk.Tk()

   root.title("Inspection Results")

   if result == 0: # Assuming 0 = Good, 1 = Defective

      message = "Part Status: Good"

      color = "green"

else:

    message = "Part Status: Defective"

    color = "red"

label = tk.Label(root, text=message, fg=color, font=("Arial", 20))

label.pack()

root.mainloop()

update_gui(final_result)

10.6 Handling Defects

Alerts

Use GPIO peripherals to signal defects:

- **Lights:** Turn on red LEDs for defective parts.
- **Speakers:** Play an audio alert.

GPIO Alert Example:

```python
import RPi.GPIO as GPIO

GPIO.setmode(GPIO.BCM)
GPIO.setup(18, GPIO.OUT)   # Red LED
GPIO.setup(23, GPIO.OUT)   # Speaker

if final_result == 1:   # Defective part
    GPIO.output(18, GPIO.HIGH)   # Turn on LED
    GPIO.output(23, GPIO.HIGH)   # Play sound
else:
    GPIO.output(18, GPIO.LOW)
    GPIO.output(23, GPIO.LOW)
```

10.7 Challenges and Solutions

Synchronization Issues

Solution: Use hardware triggers or optimize threading.

AI Model Errors

Solution: Retrain the model with more diverse images and defects.

Processing Delays

Solution: Reduce image resolution or use TensorFlow Lite for faster inference.

10.8 Enhancing Real-Time Detection

Advanced Features

1. **Defect Localization:** Highlight defect regions in the captured images.

2. **Statistical Analysis:** Track defect rates and generate reports for production optimization.

Future Technologies

1. **Edge AI:** Deploy AI models on hardware accelerators (e.g., Coral TPU) for faster processing.

2. **IoT Integration:** Enable remote monitoring and control via cloud platforms.

Conclusion

Real-time detection with multi-camera comparison is the heart of the Multiview AI Part Inspection System. By integrating synchronized imaging with AI-driven classification, the system delivers accurate and efficient defect analysis, transforming quality control in manufacturing. With this setup complete, the next chapters will explore additional features such as GPIO integration and performance optimization.

Light and Speaker Integration (GPIO Control)

Introduction

No inspection system is complete without real-time feedback mechanisms. Lights and speakers provide visual and auditory cues, making the Multiview AI Part Inspection System interactive and user-friendly. These peripherals not only enhance the operator's experience but also improve efficiency by alerting users to system states and defect detections.

This chapter walks through the integration of GPIO-controlled lights and speakers into your system. From hardware setup to software implementation, you'll learn how to configure these peripherals to respond dynamically to inspection results.

11.1 The Role of Lights and Speakers

Why Use Lights?

- **Defect Alerts:** Red lights can indicate defective parts, while green lights confirm good parts.

- **System Status:** Flashing lights can represent system readiness or errors.

Why Use Speakers?

- **Auditory Feedback:** Audio alerts provide additional cues for operators, ensuring they don't miss critical events.

- **Multilingual Announcements:** Speakers can deliver spoken messages, aligning with the system's multilingual GUI.

By combining lights and speakers, the system becomes more accessible and adaptable, particularly in noisy or visually cluttered environments.

11.2 Understanding GPIO on Raspberry Pi

The Raspberry Pi's GPIO (General Purpose Input/Output) pins allow you to interface with external hardware such as LEDs, buzzers, and relays. These pins are versatile and can be configured as input or output, making them ideal for controlling lights and speakers.

Key Features of GPIO:

- **Voltage Levels:** Operate at 3.3V logic (ensure connected peripherals are compatible).

- **Programmability:** Easily controlled using Python libraries such as RPi.GPIO.

- **Safety:** Always use resistors and appropriate circuits to protect the GPIO pins and connected devices.

11.3 Required Components

To implement light and speaker integration, you'll need:

1. **LED Lights:**

    o   Red LEDs (for defective parts).

    o   Green LEDs (for good parts).

    o   Resistors (330 ohms recommended) to limit current.

2. **Speakers or Buzzers:**

    o   Small speakers (e.g., 3W) or piezoelectric buzzers.

3. **Breadboard and Jumper Wires:** For prototyping connections.

4. **Optional Relay Module:** To control larger speakers or lights requiring higher voltage.

11.4 Wiring the Hardware

11.4.1 Connecting LEDs to GPIO Pins

1. Place the LEDs on the breadboard.

2. Connect the longer leg (anode) of the LED to a GPIO pin using a jumper wire.

3. Attach a resistor between the shorter leg (cathode) and the ground (GND) pin on the Raspberry Pi.

Example GPIO Pin Configuration:

- GPIO18: Red LED

- GPIO23: Green LED

11.4.2 Connecting the Speaker

1. Use a small speaker or buzzer that operates at 3.3V logic.

2. Connect the positive terminal to a GPIO pin and the negative terminal to GND.

3. For higher-powered speakers, use a relay module to isolate and protect the GPIO pins.

11.5 Installing Required Libraries

Install the RPi.GPIO library to control GPIO pins:

```bash
pip install RPi.GPIO
```

11.6 Writing Python Scripts for GPIO Control

11.6.1 Controlling LEDs

Use Python to turn LEDs on or off based on part inspection results.

Sample Code:

```python
import RPi.GPIO as GPIO
import time

# Set up GPIO
GPIO.setmode(GPIO.BCM)
GPIO.setup(18, GPIO.OUT)  # Red LED
GPIO.setup(23, GPIO.OUT)  # Green LED

# Simulate inspection results
def indicate_result(result):
    if result == "defective":
        GPIO.output(18, GPIO.HIGH)  # Turn on red LED
        GPIO.output(23, GPIO.LOW)   # Turn off green
    elif result == "good":
        GPIO.output(18, GPIO.LOW)
        GPIO.output(23, GPIO.HIGH)

# Test the LEDs
try:
    indicate_result("defective")
    time.sleep(2)
    indicate_result("good")
    time.sleep(2)
finally:
    GPIO.cleanup()
```

11.6.2 Playing Audio Alerts

Use the pygame library to play audio files for different events:

```bash
pip install pygame
```

Sample Code:

```python
import pygame

# Initialize pygame mixer
pygame.mixer.init()

# Load audio files
good_part_audio = "good_part.mp3"
defective_part_audio = "defective_part.mp3"

# Play audio based on result
def play_alert(result):
    if result == "good":
        pygame.mixer.music.load(good_part_audio)
    elif result == "defective":
        pygame.mixer.music.load(defective_part_audio)
    pygame.mixer.music.play()

# Test audio playback
play_alert("defective")
```

Python   Copy

11.7 Integrating Lights and Speakers with Inspection Results

Combine LED and speaker control into the inspection pipeline. After the AI model classifies a part, trigger the corresponding lights and audio.

Integration Example:

```python
def handle_inspection_result(result):
    # Control LEDs
    if result == "defective":
        GPIO.output(18, GPIO.HIGH)
        GPIO.output(23, GPIO.LOW)
        pygame.mixer.music.load("defective_part.mp3")
    elif result == "good":
        GPIO.output(18, GPIO.LOW)
        GPIO.output(23, GPIO.HIGH)
        pygame.mixer.music.load("good_part.mp3")

    # Play alert
    pygame.mixer.music.play()
```

11.8 Challenges and Troubleshooting

Issue: LEDs Not Lighting Up

Solution: Verify connections and ensure resistors are correctly placed. Use a multimeter to check voltage.

Issue: Audio Playback Delays

Solution: Preload audio files during initialization to reduce playback lag.

Issue: GPIO Warnings

Solution: Always call GPIO.cleanup() in your scripts to reset GPIO states.

11.9 Expanding the Feedback System

Multicolor RGB LEDs

Use RGB LEDs to display multiple statuses (e.g., blue for system errors).

Advanced Audio Features

- Incorporate text-to-speech (TTS) libraries for dynamic audio alerts in multiple languages:

```bash
Bash                                              Copy

pip install gTTS
```

TTS Example:

```python
Python                                            Copy

from gtts import gTTS
import os

def speak_message(message, language="en"):
    tts = gTTS(text=message, lang=language)
    tts.save("message.mp3")
    os.system("mpg321 message.mp3")

speak_message("Defective part detected!", "en")
```

Integration with GUI

Update the GUI to synchronize visual alerts with LEDs and audio notifications.

11.10 Testing and Optimization

Stress Testing

Simulate high inspection frequencies to ensure lights and speakers respond consistently under load.

Power Optimization

86

Use relays for energy-intensive peripherals to offload power from the Raspberry Pi.

Conclusion

The integration of GPIO-controlled lights and speakers transforms the Multiview AI Part Inspection System into an interactive, real-time feedback tool. By following this chapter, you've added layers of interactivity that improve the user experience, making defect detection more intuitive and actionable. These features not only enhance usability but also pave the way for further innovation, such as multilingual announcements and IoT connectivity.

Button Integration: Start Checking & Reset Counter

Introduction

Buttons serve as one of the simplest and most reliable interfaces for users to interact with an electronic system. In the Multiview AI Part Inspection System, the integration of physical buttons empowers users to control key processes: initiating the inspection cycle and resetting counters. This functionality reduces dependency on software-only controls, making the system more robust, especially in industrial environments where quick tactile inputs are often more efficient.

In this chapter, we will walk through integrating physical buttons with your Raspberry Pi. From hardware setup to implementing Python scripts for button functionality, this chapter ensures that your system is intuitive and easy to operate.

12.1 Understanding Button Functionality

Why Integrate Buttons?

1. **Convenience:** Simplifies user interaction, especially in fast-paced environments.

2. **Reliability:** Offers a tactile and responsive alternative to GUI controls.

3. **Durability:** Physical buttons are designed to withstand harsh conditions such as dirt, dust, or vibrations.

Core Functionalities

- **Start Checking:** Initiates the inspection process when pressed.

- **Reset Counter:** Resets the good and defective part counters to zero, preparing the system for a new batch of inspections.

12.2 Required Components

To integrate buttons into your system, you will need:

1. **Momentary Push Buttons:** These buttons close the circuit only while pressed, making them ideal for short-duration operations.

2. **Resistors:** Use pull-down resistors (e.g., 10k ohms) to stabilize the signal and avoid false triggering.

3. **Breadboard and Jumper Wires:** For prototyping connections.

4. **Raspberry Pi Board:** With sufficient GPIO pins for interfacing.

12.3 Wiring Buttons to GPIO Pins

Step 1: Understanding Button Circuits

Buttons are simple devices that complete a circuit when pressed. They require:

- **Power Supply:** Provided by the Raspberry Pi's 3.3V GPIO pins.

- **Pull-Down Resistors:** Ensure the GPIO pin reads a LOW (0) signal when the button is not pressed.

Step 2: Connecting the Components

1. Place the push buttons on the breadboard.

2. Connect one terminal of the button to a GPIO pin (e.g., GPIO17 for Start Checking, GPIO27 for Reset Counter).

3. Attach a pull-down resistor (10k ohm) between the same GPIO pin and GND.

4. Connect the other terminal of the button to the 3.3V power supply.

Example GPIO Pin Allocation:

- GPIO17: Start Checking button

- GPIO27: Reset Counter button

12.4 Testing Button Connections

Step 1: Installing the RPi.GPIO Library

Ensure the GPIO library is installed:

```bash
Bash                                    Copy

pip install RPi.GPIO
```

Step 2: Writing a Test Script

Use Python to test button functionality:

```python
Python                                    Copy

import RPi.GPIO as GPIO
import time

# Set up GPIO
GPIO.setmode(GPIO.BCM)
GPIO.setup(17, GPIO.IN, pull_up_down=GPIO.PUD_DOWN)
GPIO.setup(27, GPIO.IN, pull_up_down=GPIO.PUD_DOWN)

try:
    while True:
        if GPIO.input(17) == GPIO.HIGH:
            print("Start Checking button pressed")
        if GPIO.input(27) == GPIO.HIGH:
            print("Reset Counter button pressed")
        time.sleep(0.1)
finally:
    GPIO.cleanup()
```

Run this script, and press each button to verify the output in the terminal.

12.5 Implementing Button Functions in the Inspection System

12.5.1 Start Checking Functionality

The Start Checking button initiates the image capture and classification processes:

1. Detect button press using GPIO.

2. Trigger the image capture script for all cameras.

3. Perform AI inference on captured images and display results.

Sample Code:

```python
import threading
import time
import RPi.GPIO as GPIO

# Set up GPIO
GPIO.setmode(GPIO.BCM)
GPIO.setup(17, GPIO.IN, pull_up_down=GPIO.PUD_DOWN)

def start_inspection():
    print("Starting Inspection")
    # Simulate inspection logic
    time.sleep(2)
    print("Inspection Complete")

try:
    while True:
        if GPIO.input(17) == GPIO.HIGH:
            threading.Thread(target=start_inspection)
        time.sleep(0.1)
finally:
    GPIO.cleanup()
```

import threading

import time

import RPi.GPIO as GPIO

 # Set up GPIO

GPIO.setmode(GPIO.BCM)

GPIO.setup(17, GPIO.IN, pull_up_down=GPIO.PUD_DOWN) # Start Checking button

92

```
def start_inspection():
    print("Starting Inspection")
    # Simulate inspection logic
    time.sleep(2)
    print("Inspection Complete")


try:
    while True:
        if GPIO.input(17) == GPIO.HIGH:
            threading.Thread(target=start_inspection).start()
        time.sleep(0.1)
finally:
    GPIO.cleanup()
```

12.5.2 Reset Counter Functionality

The Reset Counter button resets the counters for good and defective parts to zero:

1. Detect button press using GPIO.

2. Reset the variables tracking the counters.

3. Update the GUI or display to reflect the reset values.

Sample Code:

```python
good_parts = 10
defective_parts = 5

def reset_counters():
    global good_parts, defective_parts
    good_parts = 0
    defective_parts = 0
    print("Counters Reset")

# Set up GPIO for Reset Counter button
GPIO.setup(27, GPIO.IN, pull_up_down=GPIO.PUD_DOWN)

try:
    while True:
        if GPIO.input(27) == GPIO.HIGH:
            reset_counters()
        time.sleep(0.1)
finally:
    GPIO.cleanup()
```

12.6 Integrating Buttons with the GUI

To create a seamless user experience, synchronize button functionality with the GUI. For example:

- **Start Checking Button:** Disables the Start button on the GUI while inspection is in progress.

- **Reset Counter Button:** Updates the displayed counters on the GUI in real-time.

Integration Example:

```python
import tkinter as tk

good_parts = 10
defective_parts = 5

def reset_counters_gui():
    global good_parts, defective_parts
    good_parts = 0
    defective_parts = 0
    good_label.config(text=f"Good Parts: {good_parts}
    defective_label.config(text=f"Defective Parts: {d

# GUI setup
root = tk.Tk()
root.title("Part Inspection")

good_label = tk.Label(root, text=f"Good Parts: {good_
good_label.pack()

defective_label = tk.Label(root, text=f"Defective Par
defective_label.pack()

# Update button state
root.mainloop()
```

import tkinter as tk

good_parts = 10

defective_parts = 5

def reset_counters_gui():

```
global good_parts, defective_parts

good_parts = 0

defective_parts = 0

good_label.config(text=f"Good Parts: {good_parts}")

defective_label.config(text=f"Defective Parts: {defective_parts}")


# GUI setup

root = tk.Tk()

root.title("Part Inspection")


good_label = tk.Label(root, text=f"Good Parts: {good_parts}")

good_label.pack()


defective_label = tk.Label(root, text=f"Defective Parts:
{defective_parts}")

defective_label.pack()


# Update button state

root.mainloop()
```

12.7 Troubleshooting Common Issues

Issue: Button Press Not Detected

Solution: Verify wiring and ensure the pull-down resistor is correctly connected.

Issue: Debouncing Problems

Solution: Implement software debouncing to filter out unintended signals:

```python
def is_pressed(pin):
    count = 0
    for _ in range(5):  # Sample 5 times
        if GPIO.input(pin) == GPIO.HIGH:
            count += 1
        time.sleep(0.01)
    return count >= 3
```

Issue: GPIO Warnings

Solution: Always call GPIO.cleanup() at the end of your script to reset pin states.

12.8 Enhancing Button Functionality

Using LEDs for Visual Feedback

- Attach LEDs to indicate button states (e.g., green LED for active Start Checking button).

Adding Long-Press Actions

- Assign different functions to short and long button presses:

```python
def detect_long_press(pin):
    start_time = time.time()
    while GPIO.input(pin) == GPIO.HIGH:
        pass
    press_duration = time.time() - start_time
    if press_duration > 2:
        print("Long Press Detected")
    else:
        print("Short Press Detected")
```

Incorporating Safety Mechanisms

- Prevent accidental resets by requiring the Reset Counter button to be held for 3 seconds.

12.9 Field Testing the Buttons

Once the buttons are integrated, test their functionality under real-world conditions:

1. Simulate high-frequency usage to ensure durability.

2. Evaluate tactile feedback and placement ergonomics.

3. Confirm synchronization with other system components.

Conclusion

Button integration brings an element of simplicity and reliability to the Multiview AI Part Inspection System. By configuring the Start Checking and Reset Counter buttons, you've added essential control elements that improve usability and efficiency. Whether used in a high-speed production line or a research environment, these buttons provide a tactile, user-friendly interface that complements the advanced technology within your system.

Chapter 13: Counting Good Parts and Target Notification

Introduction

Counting inspected parts and providing timely notifications about production targets are vital features of the Multiview AI Part Inspection System. These functionalities streamline operations by tracking the number of good parts produced, monitoring defective parts, and alerting users when specified targets are reached. Real-time visibility into these metrics ensures efficiency and enhances decision-making in manufacturing environments.

This chapter explains how to integrate counting mechanisms and notification systems into the inspection system. From implementing counters in software to setting up GPIO-based target alerts, you will learn how to create a robust tracking module that aligns with production goals.

13.1 Why Counting and Notifications Matter

The Importance of Part Counting

1. **Productivity Tracking:** Counting good parts provides real-time updates on throughput.

2. **Quality Assurance:** Monitoring defective parts helps identify areas for process improvement.

3. **Goal Setting:** Tracking counts against production targets keeps operations focused.

The Role of Notifications

1. **Timely Alerts:** Notify operators when targets are met or exceeded.

2. **Decision Support:** Enable data-driven adjustments to production schedules.

3. **Automation Integration:** Streamline actions such as pausing or resetting counters.

13.2 Required Components

To implement counting and notifications, you will need:

1. **Software Environment:** Python scripts for tracking counts and triggering notifications.

2. **Hardware:**

   o GPIO-connected LEDs and speakers for visual and auditory alerts.

   o Optional LCD or touchscreen display for live count updates.

13.3 Setting Up Counters in Software

Initializing Counters

Define variables to track the number of good and defective parts:

```Python
good_parts = 0
defective_parts = 0
target = 50  # Example target for good parts
```

Updating Counters

Integrate counter updates into the inspection pipeline:

```python
def update_counters(result):
    global good_parts, defective_parts
    if result == "good":
        good_parts += 1
    elif result == "defective":
        defective_parts += 1
```

Displaying Counters

Print counter values to the terminal or update the GUI:

```python
print(f"Good Parts: {good_parts}")
print(f"Defective Parts: {defective_parts}")
```

13.4 Setting Up Target Notifications

Defining Targets

Assign a production target for good parts:

```python
target = 50
```

Triggering Notifications

Check counters against the target during updates:

```python
Python                                              📋 Copy

def check_target():
    if good_parts >= target:
        print("Target reached!")
        trigger_alert()
```

13.5 Integrating GPIO-Based Alerts

Wiring LEDs for Target Notifications

Set up GPIO-connected LEDs:

1. Connect a green LED to indicate target achievement.

2. Attach a pull-down resistor (10k ohm) to stabilize the circuit.

Writing Python Scripts for Alerts

Use Python to control LEDs based on the counters:

```python
Python                                              📋 Copy

import RPi.GPIO as GPIO

# GPIO setup
GPIO.setmode(GPIO.BCM)
GPIO.setup(18, GPIO.OUT)  # Green LED for target achi

def trigger_alert():
    GPIO.output(18, GPIO.HIGH)  # Turn on LED
    print("Congratulations! Target reached.")
    time.sleep(2)  # Keep LED on for 2 seconds
    GPIO.output(18, GPIO.LOW)
```

13.6 Adding Audio Notifications

Using a Speaker for Alerts

Install the pygame library to play audio files:

```bash
pip install pygame
```

Playing Target Alerts

Play a congratulatory message when targets are met:

```python
import pygame

pygame.mixer.init()
pygame.mixer.music.load("target_reached.mp3")

def trigger_audio_alert():
    pygame.mixer.music.play()
```

13.7 Synchronizing Counters with the GUI

Updating the Display

Add real-time counter updates to the GUI:

```python
import tkinter as tk

def update_gui():
    good_label.config(text=f"Good Parts: {good_parts}
    defective_label.config(text=f"Defective Parts: {d

# GUI setup
root = tk.Tk()
root.title("Production Counters")

good_label = tk.Label(root, text=f"Good Parts: {good_
good_label.pack()

defective_label = tk.Label(root, text=f"Defective Par
defective_label.pack()

root.mainloop()
```

import tkinter as tk

def update_gui():

good_label.config(text=f"Good Parts: {good_parts}")

defective_label.config(text=f"Defective Parts: {defective_parts}")

GUI setup

root = tk.Tk()

root.title("Production Counters")

```
good_label = tk.Label(root, text=f"Good Parts: {good_parts}")

good_label.pack()


defective_label = tk.Label(root, text=f"Defective Parts:
{defective_parts}")

defective_label.pack()


root.mainloop()
```

13.8 Troubleshooting Common Issues

Counters Not Updating

Solution: Verify that counter update logic is correctly integrated into the inspection pipeline.

LED or Speaker Alerts Not Triggering

Solution: Check GPIO wiring and test individual alerts with a simple script.

GUI Lag During Counter Updates

Solution: Optimize GUI code by minimizing redraws and using efficient data handling methods.

13.9 Enhancing Counting and Notifications

Advanced Features

1. **Dynamic Targets:** Allow users to set and update production targets through the GUI.

2. **Statistical Tracking:** Log counter values over time for trend analysis.

Hardware Upgrades

1. **LCD Displays:** Use a small LCD screen to show counters and progress bars.

2. **Buzzer Alerts:** Add buzzers for high-priority notifications.

Conclusion

By implementing counters and target notifications, the Multiview AI Part Inspection System becomes more efficient and user-friendly. With these features in place, operators can easily track production progress, identify bottlenecks, and celebrate milestones, all while maintaining focus on quality. These additions enhance the system's overall functionality, paving the way for greater adaptability in real-world applications.

Chapter 14: Defect Naming and Audio Alert System

Introduction

Effective defect management is key to maintaining quality standards in manufacturing. The ability to categorize and name defects, combined with audio alerts for immediate recognition, transforms the inspection process into a proactive mechanism. This chapter focuses on implementing defect naming capabilities and an audio alert system into the Multiview AI Part Inspection System. These features make defect detection more user-friendly and actionable, enabling operators to respond quickly and confidently.

With the integration of these capabilities, users not only receive visual notifications but also benefit from organized defect categorization and auditory cues that ensure critical issues are never overlooked.

14.1 Defect Categorization: Why It Matters

The Role of Defect Naming

Categorizing defects and assigning specific names to them creates clarity in reporting and analysis:

1. **Improved Traceability:** Identified defects can be logged for long-term analysis.

2. **Enhanced Accuracy:** Specific names reduce ambiguity, ensuring operators know what action to take.

3. **Streamlined Communication:** Teams can quickly convey issues using clear defect labels.

Common Defect Examples

1. **Surface Crack:** Indicates visible cracks or fractures on part surfaces.

2. **Misalignment:** Suggests parts are incorrectly positioned or assembled.

3. **Color Anomaly:** Refers to discoloration or incorrect finishes.

Naming defects allows the system to evolve with your manufacturing needs, adapting to new defect types over time.

14.2 Implementing Defect Naming in Software

Step 1: Extending the AI Model for Defect Classification

Modify the AI model to categorize defects based on uploaded training images. Instead of binary classification (good/defective), the model now predicts specific defect types.

Example: Updating AI Model Outputs

1. Modify the model architecture to output multiple classes:

```python
model = Sequential([
    Conv2D(32, (3, 3), activation='relu', input_shape=(224, 224, 3)),
    MaxPooling2D(pool_size=(2, 2)),
    Conv2D(64, (3, 3), activation='relu'),
    MaxPooling2D(pool_size=(2, 2)),
    Flatten(),
    Dense(128, activation='relu'),
    Dense(5, activation='softmax')  # Assuming five defect categories
])
```

2. Retrain the model with labeled images of specific defect types, ensuring it can identify Surface Cracks, Misalignments, etc.

Step 2: Mapping Predictions to Names

Link numerical predictions to defect names:

```python
def map_prediction_to_defect(prediction):
    defect_labels = {
        0: "Surface Crack",
        1: "Misalignment",
        2: "Color Anomaly",
        3: "Shape Deformation",
        4: "Missing Part"
    }
    return defect_labels[prediction]
```

Step 3: Displaying Defect Names

Update the GUI to show defect names alongside inspection results:

```python
def update_gui_with_defect(defect_name):
    defect_label.config(text=f"Defect: {defect_name}")
```

14.3 Integrating Audio Alerts

Step 1: Selecting Alert Types

Audio alerts can vary based on the defect:

1. **Critical Alert:** Play an urgent tone for major defects (e.g., missing parts).

2. **Warning Alert:** Use a softer tone for minor issues (e.g., color anomalies).

Step 2: Preparing Audio Files

Pre-record audio messages corresponding to each defect:

- Example files: surface_crack.mp3, misalignment.mp3.

Step 3: Playing Alerts Using Python

Use the pygame library for audio playback:

109

```python
import pygame

pygame.mixer.init()

def play_defect_alert(defect_name):
    audio_files = {
        "Surface Crack": "surface_crack.mp3",
        "Misalignment": "misalignment.mp3",
        "Color Anomaly": "color_anomaly.mp3",
        "Shape Deformation": "shape_deformation.mp3",
        "Missing Part": "missing_part.mp3"
    }
    pygame.mixer.music.load(audio_files[defect_name])
    pygame.mixer.music.play()
```

14.4 Synchronizing Audio Alerts and Defect Names

Combine defect naming and audio alerts into the inspection pipeline:

```python
def handle_defect(result):
    defect_name = map_prediction_to_defect(result)
    update_gui_with_defect(defect_name)
    play_defect_alert(defect_name)
```

14.5 Challenges and Troubleshooting

Issue: AI Model Misclassifications

Solution: Expand the dataset with more images of specific defect types to improve model accuracy.

Issue: Delayed Audio Alerts

Solution: Preload audio files into memory to reduce playback latency.

Issue: Defect Names Not Displayed

Solution: Verify GUI update logic and ensure defect names are mapped correctly.

14.6 Enhancing Defect Naming and Audio Alerts

Feature 1: Dynamic Updates

Allow users to add new defect categories and upload corresponding audio files through the GUI.

Example GUI Integration:

```python
import tkinter as tk
from tkinter import filedialog

def add_new_defect_category():
    new_category = input("Enter new defect name:")
    new_audio_file = filedialog.askopenfilename(title="Select Audio File")
    defect_labels.append(new_category)
    audio_files[new_category] = new_audio_file
```

Feature 2: Multilingual Audio Alerts

Integrate text-to-speech libraries for multilingual audio alerts:

```python
from gtts import gTTS
import os

def speak_alert(defect_name, language="en"):
    message = f"{defect_name} detected!"
    tts = gTTS(text=message, lang=language)
    tts.save("alert.mp3")
    os.system("mpg321 alert.mp3")
```

Feature 3: Statistical Tracking

Log defect occurrences and generate reports for trend analysis:

```python
def log_defect(defect_name):
    with open("defect_log.txt", "a") as log_file:
        log_file.write(f"{defect_name} detected at {time.ctime()}\n")
```

14.7 Field Testing and Optimization

Testing Audio Alerts

Conduct trials in noisy environments to ensure audio alerts are audible and clear.

Testing Defect Categorization

Validate AI model accuracy against real-world defect samples.

Conclusion

Integrating defect naming and audio alerts elevates the Multiview AI Part Inspection System from functional to intuitive and proactive. These features enhance the user experience by offering clear categorization and immediate recognition of issues, enabling swift corrective action. As a result, the system becomes a cornerstone of quality assurance, delivering valuable insights into manufacturing processes while empowering operators to maintain high standards.

Chapter 15: Language Switching for GUI and Speaker

Introduction

Global deployment of the Multiview AI Part Inspection System requires adaptability to diverse linguistic and cultural needs. Language switching functionality in both the graphical user interface (GUI) and audio alert system ensures accessibility for operators worldwide, reducing training time and improving usability. With this capability, users can interact with the system in their preferred language, making it inclusive and effective across various regions.

This chapter focuses on implementing multilingual support for the GUI and speaker announcements. By the end of this chapter, the system will dynamically toggle between languages, enabling operators to choose their desired language seamlessly.

15.1 The Importance of Multilingual Support

Why Language Switching Matters

1. **Inclusivity:** Enables operators who speak different languages to use the system efficiently.

2. **Global Scalability:** Makes the system deployable across factories in various countries.

3. **Error Reduction:** Improves comprehension and minimizes errors during operation.

Areas of Multilingual Integration

1. GUI Text: Labels, buttons, menus, and notifications displayed on the interface.

2. Audio Alerts: Spoken announcements for defect alerts and system states.

3. Logs and Reports: Optional translation of logs for multilingual documentation.

15.2 Setting Up Language Switching in the GUI

Step 1: Storing Language Data

Store text translations in JSON files for easy management and scalability. Each JSON file represents a language.

Example JSON Files: en.json:

```json
{
    "start_button": "Start Inspection",
    "reset_button": "Reset Counters",
    "good_parts_label": "Good Parts",
    "defective_parts_label": "Defective Parts",
    "language_label": "Select Language"
}
```

fr.json:

```json
{
    "start_button": "Démarrer l'inspection",
    "reset_button": "Réinitialiser les compteurs",
    "good_parts_label": "Pièces Correctes",
    "defective_parts_label": "Pièces Défaut",
    "language_label": "Choisir la langue"
}
```

Step 2: Loading Language Data

Write a function to load the selected language file:

```python
import json

def load_language(language_code):
    with open(f"{language_code}.json", "r") as file:
        return json.load(file)
```

Step 3: Updating GUI Text

Create a function to update all GUI elements dynamically based on the selected language:

```python
def update_language(language_data):
    start_button.config(text=language_data["start_button"])
    reset_button.config(text=language_data["reset_button"])
    good_label.config(text=language_data["good_parts_label"])
    defective_label.config(text=language_data["defective_parts_label"])
```

Step 4: Adding a Language Selector

Include a dropdown menu in the GUI to allow users to select their preferred language:

```python
import tkinter as tk
from tkinter import ttk

def change_language(event):
    selected_language = language_var.get()
    language_data = load_language(selected_language)
    update_language(language_data)

# Initialize GUI
root = tk.Tk()
root.title("Multiview AI Part Inspection")

language_var = tk.StringVar(value="en")
languages = {"English": "en", "French": "fr"}
language_dropdown = ttk.Combobox(root, values=list(languages.keys()))
language_dropdown.pack()
language_dropdown.bind("<<ComboboxSelected>>", change_language)

# GUI Elements
start_button = tk.Button(root, text="Start Inspection")
start_button.pack()

reset_button = tk.Button(root, text="Reset Counters")
reset_button.pack()

good_label = tk.Label(root, text="Good Parts: 0")
good_label.pack()

defective_label = tk.Label(root, text="Defective Parts: 0")
defective_label.pack()

# Main Loop
root.mainloop()
```

15.3 Integrating Multilingual Audio Alerts

Step 1: Preparing Audio Files

Record audio alerts for each language and save them with descriptive filenames:

- good_part_en.mp3, good_part_fr.mp3

- defective_part_en.mp3, defective_part_fr.mp3

Step 2: Managing Audio Alerts

Map each defect type and system event to audio files for multiple languages:

```python
audio_files = {
    "en": {
        "good_part": "good_part_en.mp3",
        "defective_part": "defective_part_en.mp3"
    },
    "fr": {
        "good_part": "good_part_fr.mp3",
        "defective_part": "defective_part_fr.mp3"
    }
}
```

Step 3: Playing the Correct Audio File

Based on the selected language and alert type, play the corresponding audio file:

```python
import pygame

pygame.mixer.init()

def play_audio_alert(alert_type, language_code):
    file_path = audio_files[language_code][alert_type]
    pygame.mixer.music.load(file_path)
    pygame.mixer.music.play()
```

Step 4: Testing Audio Alerts

Simulate events to test audio alerts in different languages:

python

```python
play_audio_alert("good_part", "en")
play_audio_alert("defective_part", "fr")
```

15.4 Challenges and Troubleshooting

Issue: Missing Translations

Solution: Implement fallback logic to default to English if a translation is unavailable:

```python
def load_language_with_fallback(language_code):
    try:
        return load_language(language_code)
    except FileNotFoundError:
        print(f"Language file not found for {language_code}. Defaulting to E
        return load_language("en")
```

Issue: Audio Playback Errors

Solution: Verify file paths and ensure audio files are encoded in a compatible format (e.g., MP3 or WAV).

Issue: GUI Lag During Language Switching

Solution: Use efficient update logic to avoid redundant redraws of GUI elements.

15.5 Enhancing Multilingual Functionality

Dynamic Language Addition

Allow administrators to upload new translations and audio files through a management interface:

```python
def add_language():
    new_language = input("Enter the new language code:")
    # Save new JSON file and corresponding audio files
```

Automatic Language Detection

Detect the user's language preference based on system settings or IP geolocation.

Multilingual Logs

Translate system logs and reports for multilingual documentation:

```python
Python                                                    Copy

def translate_log_entry(entry, language_code):
    # Use a translation API for dynamic log translation
    pass
```

15.6 Field Testing Multilingual Features

1. **Language Accessibility Testing:**

   o Verify GUI and audio alerts for each supported language.

   o Test usability in real-world scenarios with diverse operators.

2. **Error Handling Testing:**

   o Check behavior when language files or audio alerts are missing.

   o Ensure fallback mechanisms function as intended.

3. **User Feedback:**

   o Gather operator feedback on language accuracy and ease of use.

   o Adjust translations and pronunciations for local dialects if needed.

Conclusion

Language switching in the GUI and speaker enhances the Multiview AI Part Inspection System's versatility, allowing it to adapt to a global audience. By providing seamless multilingual support, the system becomes a valuable tool for diverse teams and manufacturing environments, ensuring accessibility and efficiency. With this chapter completed, your inspection system is ready to thrive in multilingual settings, setting the stage for global deployment and success.

Chapter 16: Weekly Auto-Retraining with New Images

Introduction

The Multiview AI Part Inspection System's performance hinges on the accuracy of its AI model. Regular updates to the model ensure that it adapts to new part variations, defect types, and environmental changes. A weekly auto-retraining feature, leveraging new images captured during inspections, keeps the model fresh and effective. By automating this process, the system achieves continuous improvement with minimal human intervention.

This chapter explains how to implement weekly auto-retraining, covering everything from data collection to model deployment. By the end of this chapter, your system will have a built-in mechanism for learning from real-world data, guaranteeing long-term reliability and scalability.

16.1 The Importance of Auto-Retraining

Benefits of Auto-Retraining

1. **Adaptability:** Incorporates new defect types and part variations into the model.

2. **Improved Accuracy:** Enhances detection rates by expanding the dataset regularly.

3. **Automation:** Reduces the need for manual retraining, saving time and resources.

Challenges Addressed

- Outdated models that fail to recognize uncommon defects.

- The need for scalable, hands-free maintenance in high-production environments.

16.2 Workflow Overview

The weekly auto-retraining process involves the following steps:

1. **Data Collection:** Images of inspected parts are saved with labels (good/defective).

2. **Data Preprocessing:** Uploaded images are cleaned, normalized, and organized.

3. **Model Training:** The updated dataset is used to retrain the AI model.

4. **Testing and Validation:** The new model is evaluated to ensure performance improvements.

5. **Deployment:** The retrained model replaces the old one in the live system.

16.3 Automating Data Collection

Step 1: Saving Inspection Images

Modify the image capture script to save images into labeled folders:

```python
import os
import cv2

def save_inspection_image(result, image, part_id):
    folder = "Good_Parts" if result == "good" else "Defective_Parts"
    os.makedirs(folder, exist_ok=True)
    filename = os.path.join(folder, f"{part_id}.jpg")
    cv2.imwrite(filename, image)
```

Images captured by the cameras are automatically saved with labels based on inspection results.

Step 2: Organizing Data

Separate data by week to ensure retraining uses the most recent samples:

122

```python
import shutil

def organize_data_weekly():
    current_week_folder = "Dataset_Week_X"
    shutil.move("Good_Parts", f"{current_week_folder}/Good_Parts")
    shutil.move("Defective_Parts", f"{current_week_folder}/Defective_Parts")
```

Run this function every week using a scheduled task.

16.4 Preprocessing Data

Step 1: Cleaning and Filtering Images

Remove duplicate or blurry images to ensure quality:

```python
import cv2

def filter_images(image_folder):
    for filename in os.listdir(image_folder):
        image = cv2.imread(os.path.join(image_folder, filename))
        if image is None or is_blurry(image):
            os.remove(os.path.join(image_folder, filename))

def is_blurry(image):
    gray_image = cv2.cvtColor(image, cv2.COLOR_BGR2GRAY)
    return cv2.Laplacian(gray_image).var() < 100
```

Step 2: Normalizing and Resizing

Prepare images for model input by resizing and normalizing them:

```python
def preprocess_image(image_path):
    image = cv2.imread(image_path)
    resized = cv2.resize(image, (224, 224))
    normalized = resized / 255.0
    return normalized
```

16.5 Retraining the AI Model

Step 1: Loading the Dataset

Load the newly organized dataset for training:

```python
from tensorflow.keras.preprocessing.image import ImageDataGenerator

datagen = ImageDataGenerator(validation_split=0.2)  # 20% for validation
train_generator = datagen.flow_from_directory(
    "Dataset_Week_X",
    target_size=(224, 224),
    batch_size=32,
    class_mode="categorical",
    subset="training"
)
validation_generator = datagen.flow_from_directory(
    "Dataset_Week_X",
    target_size=(224, 224),
    batch_size=32,
    class_mode="categorical",
    subset="validation"
)
```

Step 2: Retraining the Model

Use the new dataset to retrain the AI model:

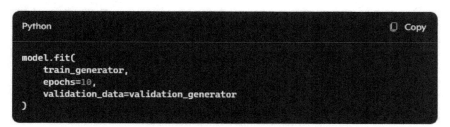

```python
model.fit(
    train_generator,
    epochs=10,
    validation_data=validation_generator
)
```

Step 3: Saving the Retrained Model

Save the updated model for deployment:

```python
model.save("updated_part_inspection_model.h5")
```

124

16.6 Testing and Validating the Retrained Model

Step 1: Evaluating Accuracy

Assess the model's performance using the validation set:

```python
test_loss, test_accuracy = model.evaluate(validation_generator)
print(f"Validation Accuracy: {test_accuracy}")
```

Step 2: Comparing Results

Compare the retrained model's accuracy to the previous model to ensure improvement:

```python
previous_accuracy = 0.95  # Example previous accuracy
if test_accuracy > previous_accuracy:
    print("Retrained model performs better!")
else:
    print("Retrained model needs further adjustment.")
```

16.7 Deploying the Retrained Model

Automating Deployment

Replace the live model with the updated version:

```python
import shutil

def deploy_model():
    shutil.move("updated_part_inspection_model.h5", "/path/to/live/model/")
    print("Model successfully deployed!")
```

Testing Deployment

Run a few inspection cycles to test the live model:

```Python
def test_live_model():
    # Perform inspection with updated model
    pass
```

16.8 Scheduling Weekly Auto-Retraining

Use a scheduler to automate retraining tasks:

- **Cron Jobs (Linux):** Schedule scripts for data organization and retraining.

```Bash
0 0 * * 7 python organize_data_weekly.py
0 1 * * 7 python retrain_model.py
```

- **Task Scheduler (Windows):** Set weekly triggers for scripts.

16.9 Challenges and Troubleshooting

Issue: Insufficient Data

Solution: Expand data collection or supplement the dataset with synthetic images (e.g., using data augmentation).

Issue: Slow Training

Solution: Reduce image resolution or batch size during training.

Issue: Model Degradation

Solution: Include a validation step to prevent deploying underperforming models.

16.10 Optimizing Auto-Retraining

Feature 1: Adaptive Training Frequency

Analyze defect trends to adjust retraining frequency dynamically:

126

```python
def adjust_frequency_based_on_trends():
    if defect_rate > threshold:
        schedule_retraining_weekly()
    else:
        schedule_retraining_monthly()
```

Feature 2: Incremental Learning

Use transfer learning to retain the original model's knowledge while adding new features:

```python
model = load_model("previous_model.h5")
model.fit(new_data, epochs=5)
```

Conclusion

Weekly auto-retraining with new images ensures the Multiview AI Part Inspection System remains effective and adaptable. By automating the entire process, from data collection to model deployment, the system learns continuously, improving over time with minimal operator intervention. This chapter equips you with the tools to implement a sustainable retraining mechanism, paving the way for long-term success in quality control.

Chapter 17: Saving Logs Locally and Syncing to Google Drive

Introduction

Data logging is an integral aspect of the Multiview AI Part Inspection System, enabling comprehensive tracking of inspections, defect occurrences, and system behavior. Saving logs locally provides instant access for review and troubleshooting, while syncing these logs to Google Drive ensures secure backup, easy sharing, and accessibility across devices. Combined, these functionalities provide a reliable and scalable data management system.

This chapter dives into the methods for implementing local log storage and automatic syncing to Google Drive. From designing a structured logging system to integrating cloud synchronization, you will learn how to create a robust solution for storing and managing system-generated data effectively.

17.1 The Importance of Logging and Cloud Sync

Why Log Data Locally?

1. **Traceability:** Maintain a record of inspections and defects for future reference and audits.

2. **Troubleshooting:** Identify patterns in defects or system errors to optimize performance.

3. **Compliance:** Satisfy regulatory requirements for quality control documentation.

Why Use Cloud Sync?

1. **Backup:** Protect against data loss caused by hardware failure or system crashes.

2. **Remote Access:** Allow stakeholders to review logs from anywhere.

3. **Collaboration:** Share data across teams easily, promoting informed decision-making.

17.2 Structuring the Logging System

Types of Logs

1. **Inspection Logs:** Record details about each part inspected, including timestamps, results, and defect types.

2. **System Logs:** Capture system activity such as errors, warnings, and maintenance events.

3. **Performance Logs:** Monitor metrics like inspection speed, model accuracy, and processing times.

Log Format

Save logs in a structured and standardized format, such as CSV or JSON.

Example CSV Log:

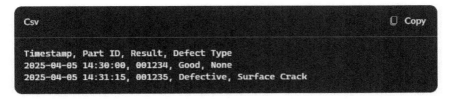

```
Csv                                              Copy

Timestamp, Part ID, Result, Defect Type
2025-04-05 14:30:00, 001234, Good, None
2025-04-05 14:31:15, 001235, Defective, Surface Crack
```

Example JSON Log:

```json
{
    "timestamp": "2025-04-05 14:31:15",
    "part_id": "001235",
    "result": "Defective",
    "defect_type": "Surface Crack"
}
```

17.3 Implementing Local Logging

Step 1: Creating a Log File

Initialize a log file at system startup:

```python
import csv

log_file = "inspection_logs.csv"

with open(log_file, mode="w", newline="") as file:
    writer = csv.writer(file)
    writer.writerow(["Timestamp", "Part ID", "Result", "Defect Type"])
```

Step 2: Writing to the Log

Append data to the log file during inspections:

```python
from datetime import datetime

def log_inspection(part_id, result, defect_type):
    timestamp = datetime.now().strftime("%Y-%m-%d %H:%M:%S")
    with open(log_file, mode="a", newline="") as file:
        writer = csv.writer(file)
        writer.writerow([timestamp, part_id, result, defect_type])
```

Step 3: Testing the Logging System

Simulate inspections and verify log entries:

```python
log_inspection("001234", "Good", "None")
log_inspection("001235", "Defective", "Surface Crack")
```

17.4 Setting Up Google Drive Integration

Step 1: Installing Google Drive API

Install the google-api-python-client and google-auth libraries:

```bash
pip install google-api-python-client google-auth google-auth-oauthlib google
```

pip install google-api-python-client google-auth google-auth-oauthlib google-auth-httplib2

Step 2: Configuring Google Drive API

1. Visit the Google Cloud Console.

2. Create a new project and enable the Google Drive API.

3. Generate OAuth 2.0 credentials and download the credentials.json file.

Step 3: Authenticating the Application

```python
from google.oauth2 import service_account
from googleapiclient.discovery import build

SCOPES = ["https://www.googleapis.com/auth/drive.file"]
SERVICE_ACCOUNT_FILE = "credentials.json"

credentials = service_account.Credentials.from_service_account_file(
    SERVICE_ACCOUNT_FILE, scopes=SCOPES
)
drive_service = build("drive", "v3", credentials=credentials)
```

17.5 Syncing Logs to Google Drive

Step 1: Uploading the Log File

Define a function to upload the log file to Google Drive:

```python
def upload_to_drive(file_path, folder_id=None):
    file_metadata = {"name": file_path.split("/")[-1]}
    if folder_id:
        file_metadata["parents"] = [folder_id]

    media = MediaFileUpload(file_path, mimetype="text/csv")
    drive_service.files().create(
        body=file_metadata, media_body=media, fields="id"
    ).execute()
    print(f"{file_path} uploaded successfully.")
```

Step 2: Automating Sync

Schedule periodic uploads to Google Drive:

```python
import threading

def auto_sync():
    upload_to_drive(log_file)
    threading.Timer(3600, auto_sync).start()  # Sync every hour

auto_sync()
```

17.6 Advanced Features

Real-Time Sync

Implement real-time sync by uploading logs immediately after updates:

132

```python
def log_and_sync(part_id, result, defect_type):
    log_inspection(part_id, result, defect_type)
    upload_to_drive(log_file)
```

Historical Data Management

Archive older logs to avoid excessive clutter:

```python
def archive_logs():
    archive_folder = "Archived_Logs"
    os.makedirs(archive_folder, exist_ok=True)
    shutil.move(log_file, f"{archive_folder}/{datetime.now().strftime('%Y-%m
```

def archive_logs():

  archive_folder = "Archived_Logs"

  os.makedirs(archive_folder, exist_ok=True)

  shutil.move(log_file, f"{archive_folder}/{datetime.now().strftime('%Y-%m-%d')}.csv")

Error Handling

Handle API errors gracefully:

```python
try:
    upload_to_drive(log_file)
except Exception as e:
    print(f"Failed to upload log: {e}")
```

17.7 Testing and Validation

Verifying Local Logs

1. Inspect log files for accuracy and completeness.

2. Test edge cases, such as empty defect types or long part IDs.

Verifying Google Drive Sync

1. Check that files appear in the correct Drive folder.

2. Test file accessibility across devices.

Stress Testing

Simulate high-frequency logging and syncing to evaluate performance under load.

17.8 Troubleshooting Common Issues

Issue: Missing Logs

Solution: Ensure the log file is opened in append mode and verify file permissions.

Issue: API Quota Limits

Solution: Optimize sync frequency and avoid redundant uploads.

Issue: Authentication Errors

Solution: Regenerate OAuth credentials and verify the service account configuration.

Conclusion

By integrating local logging and Google Drive sync, the Multiview AI Part Inspection System gains robust data storage capabilities, ensuring traceability, reliability, and accessibility. This chapter equips you to build a scalable logging system that supports operations and future growth. With these features in place, you're prepared for real-world challenges in data management and quality assurance.

Chapter 18: Auto-Start GUI on Boot (Touchscreen Support)

Introduction

For an automated system such as the Multiview AI Part Inspection System, it's essential that the interface becomes operational immediately upon system startup. This eliminates the need for manual initialization, particularly in fast-paced or production-focused environments. Adding a touchscreen display as a primary control interface simplifies the operation further, making the system user-friendly and easily accessible without reliance on external devices like keyboards or mice.

In this chapter, we will guide you through setting up your Raspberry Pi to automatically launch the GUI application on boot. Additionally, we'll cover optimizing the GUI for touchscreen devices to ensure seamless user interaction. By the end of this chapter, you'll have a fully self-sufficient system that boots directly into an accessible and intuitive interface.

18.1 Why Auto-Start GUI Is Essential

Key Benefits

1. **Ease of Use:** Ensures that operators can immediately interact with the system after powering it on.

2. **Time-Saving:** Reduces downtime by skipping manual startup procedures.

3. **Error Prevention:** Minimizes the chance of user errors during the startup process.

4. **Touchscreen Accessibility:** Simplifies navigation, particularly in environments where space or resources are limited.

18.2 Setting Up the Touchscreen Display

Step 1: Hardware Connection

If you're using an official Raspberry Pi touchscreen display or a third-party touchscreen:

1. Attach the ribbon cable from the display to the Raspberry Pi's DSI (Display Serial Interface) port.

2. Connect the power wires from the display to the Raspberry Pi GPIO pins.

3. Ensure the display is powered on and functional by booting the Raspberry Pi.

Step 2: Calibrating the Touchscreen

Some touchscreens may require calibration to ensure accuracy:

1. Install the xinput-calibrator tool:

```Bash
sudo apt install xinput-calibrator
```

2. Launch the calibration utility:

```Bash
sudo apt install xinput-calibrator
```

3. Follow the on-screen instructions and save the generated configuration.

18.3 Configuring Auto-Start for the GUI

Step 1: Creating a Desktop Entry

Use a desktop entry file to define the behavior of the GUI application during startup.

1. Create a .desktop file for your GUI:

```bash
sudo nano /etc/xdg/autostart/inspection_system_gui.desktop
```

2. Add the following configuration:

```ini
[Desktop Entry]
Type=Application
Name=Inspection System GUI
Exec=python3 /path/to/your/gui_script.py
X-GNOME-Autostart-enabled=true
```

Step 2: Testing the Auto-Start Configuration

1. Reboot the Raspberry Pi:

```bash
sudo reboot
```

2. Verify that the GUI application launches automatically upon startup.

18.4 Enhancing the GUI for Touchscreen Use

Step 1: Designing a Touch-Friendly Interface

To optimize the GUI for touchscreen devices:

1. **Larger Buttons:** Ensure buttons are large enough to be tapped easily.

2. **Minimalistic Design:** Avoid clutter by focusing on essential elements.

3. **Spacing:** Add sufficient padding between interactive components.

Example Button Configuration (Tkinter):

```python
import tkinter as tk

root = tk.Tk()
root.geometry("800x480")  # Set resolution for touchscreen

start_button = tk.Button(root, text="Start Inspection", width=20, height=2,
start_button.pack(pady=10)

reset_button = tk.Button(root, text="Reset Counters", width=20, height=2, fc
reset_button.pack(pady=10)

root.mainloop()
```

import tkinter as tk

root = tk.Tk()

root.geometry("800x480") # Set resolution for touchscreen

start_button = tk.Button(root, text="Start Inspection", width=20, height=2, font=("Arial", 14))

start_button.pack(pady=10)

reset_button = tk.Button(root, text="Reset Counters", width=20, height=2, font=("Arial", 14))

reset_button.pack(pady=10)

root.mainloop()

Step 2: Adding Touch Gestures

Enhance interactivity by enabling swipe or tap gestures:

1. Use tkinter or third-party libraries like Kivy for advanced gestures.

2. Assign gestures to specific system actions (e.g., swipe left to navigate logs, swipe right to change settings).

18.5 Optimizing Startup Time

Step 1: Reducing Boot Time

1. Disable unnecessary services:

```bash
sudo systemctl disable <service_name>
```

2. Enable fast boot mode in the Raspberry Pi configuration tool:

```bash
sudo raspi-config
```

Navigate to **Boot Options** and enable console auto-login.

Step 2: Monitoring System Resources

Use the htop tool to monitor resource usage and identify potential bottlenecks:

```bash
sudo apt install htop
htop
```

18.6 Implementing Error Handling

Step 1: Detecting Application Crashes

Use a watchdog script to restart the GUI if it crashes:

```bash
#!/bin/bash
while true; do
    python3 /path/to/your/gui_script.py
    sleep 5
done
```

Save this as gui_watchdog.sh and add it to your startup configuration:

```bash
sudo nano /etc/rc.local
```

Add the following line before exit 0:

```bash
bash /path/to/gui_watchdog.sh &
```

Step 2: Logging Errors

Log GUI errors for debugging:

```python
try:
    # Main GUI application logic
    root.mainloop()
except Exception as e:
    with open("gui_error_log.txt", "a") as log_file:
        log_file.write(f"{datetime.now()}: {e}\n")
```

18.7 Customizing Boot Appearance

Hiding Boot Text

Modify the cmdline.txt file to hide system messages during startup:

1. Open the file for editing:

```bash
sudo nano /boot/cmdline.txt
```

2. Add quiet splash to the end of the line.

Displaying a Splash Screen

Install plymouth to show a custom splash screen:

1. Install the tool:

```bash
sudo apt install plymouth plymouth-themes
```

2. Create a custom theme or use a preinstalled one.

3. Set the splash screen as default:

```bash
sudo plymouth-set-default-theme <theme_name>
sudo update-initramfs -u
```

18.8 Testing and Validation

Testing Auto-Start

1. Power cycle the Raspberry Pi to test startup behavior.

2. Simulate scenarios like power outages to ensure reliability.

Testing Touchscreen Responsiveness

1. Interact with all GUI elements using the touchscreen.

2. Test gestures and ensure smooth navigation.

Testing Error Handling

1. Introduce simulated errors to verify the watchdog script.

2. Check the error log for proper recording.

18.9 Future Enhancements

Advanced Touchscreen Features

1. **Virtual Keyboard:** Add an on-screen keyboard for data entry.

2. **Multi-Touch Support:** Enable zooming or scrolling gestures for enhanced interaction.

Mobile Device Integration

Enable remote operation via a mobile app, mirroring the touchscreen GUI.

Conclusion

Implementing auto-start for the GUI and optimizing it for touchscreen devices transforms the Multiview AI Part Inspection System into an intuitive, ready-to-use tool. These features streamline operations, enhance user experience, and eliminate the need for external peripherals. With the foundation laid in this chapter, the system is poised for seamless deployment in any manufacturing environment.

Chapter 19: Field Testing and Optimization

Introduction

With the Multiview AI Part Inspection System built and configured, field testing represents the crucial next step. This stage verifies that the system performs as intended under real-world conditions and allows for iterative refinements based on observations and data. Field testing assesses all facets of the system, from hardware stability and AI accuracy to user interface effectiveness and operational throughput.

In this chapter, you'll learn how to conduct comprehensive field tests, identify areas for optimization, and refine the system to meet both performance and usability goals. By methodically evaluating the system in its intended environment, you ensure it meets the rigorous demands of industrial applications.

19.1 Setting Goals for Field Testing

Objectives

1. **Validate System Performance:** Ensure cameras, AI models, and all hardware components operate seamlessly.

2. **Identify Weaknesses:** Detect bottlenecks, accuracy issues, or usability challenges that need addressing.

3. **Gather Data for Optimization:** Collect quantitative and qualitative feedback to refine the system.

Key Metrics

- **Inspection Speed:** Time taken to inspect a single part and overall throughput.

- **Defect Detection Rate:** Accuracy in identifying good parts and various defect types.

- **System Uptime:** Stability of hardware and software over prolonged use.

- **User Feedback:** Operator satisfaction with the interface, responsiveness, and overall experience.

19.2 Preparing for Field Testing

Step 1: Selecting the Testing Environment

Choose a real-world operational setting, such as a production line or quality control station, that reflects the system's intended use. Ensure:

1. Adequate lighting and workspace for cameras and hardware.

2. Power sources and network connectivity (if required).

Step 2: Simulating Production Conditions

Use a diverse set of test parts to simulate actual production scenarios:

1. Include both "good" parts and known defective parts with various defect types.

2. Vary part sizes, materials, and orientations to test the system's adaptability.

Step 3: Preparing Logging Tools

Set up detailed logging for all inspections during testing:

- Capture timestamps, inspection results, and defect classifications.

- Log hardware and software errors for analysis.

19.3 Conducting Initial Tests

Step 1: Verifying Hardware

1. Inspect camera alignment and ensure all angles are covered.

2. Confirm that GPIO peripherals (lights, buttons, speakers) respond appropriately.

3. Monitor the Raspberry Pi's temperature and resource utilization during operation.

Step 2: Running the Inspection Pipeline

1. Start the system using the auto-start GUI configured in Chapter 18.

2. Run a set of test parts through the inspection process.

3. Observe and record outcomes for:

   o Inspection speed.

   o Classification accuracy.

   o Responsiveness of notifications and alerts.

Step 3: Collecting Initial Data

Analyze inspection results to assess performance:

- **Accuracy:** Compare the system's classifications to ground truth data (e.g., known defect types).

- **Throughput:** Measure the number of parts inspected per hour.

- **Error Logs:** Review any issues captured during the test.

19.4 Common Issues and Troubleshooting

Issue 1: Poor Image Quality

Symptom: Blurry, dark, or overexposed images from the cameras.
Solution:

1. Adjust camera focus and brightness settings.

2. Add LED lighting or use diffusers to eliminate shadows and glare.

145

Issue 2: Misclassification by AI

Symptom: AI model incorrectly labels good parts as defective or vice versa. **Solution:**

1. Retrain the model with additional images, focusing on edge cases.

2. Verify preprocessing steps, such as image resizing and normalization.

Issue 3: Slow Inspection Speed

Symptom: System struggles to process parts quickly enough to meet throughput requirements. **Solution:**

1. Optimize AI inference by using TensorFlow Lite or other lightweight frameworks.

2. Reduce image resolution or batch processing size.

Issue 4: System Crashes

Symptom: Raspberry Pi becomes unresponsive during testing. **Solution:**

1. Use a heatsink or cooling fan to prevent overheating.

2. Monitor CPU usage and disable unnecessary background services.

19.5 Optimizing Performance

Hardware Optimizations

1. **Camera Upgrades:** Replace lower-resolution cameras with high-definition models.

2. **Lighting Improvements:** Add dynamic lighting that adjusts based on part reflectivity or material.

3. **Power Supply:** Use a stable power source with a UPS to prevent interruptions.

Software Optimizations

1. **Parallel Processing:** Implement multithreading to handle image capture and classification concurrently.

2. **Reduced Latency:** Optimize GPIO control and notification triggers to ensure near-instant response.

3. **Error Handling:** Enhance robustness by gracefully recovering from hardware or software failures.

19.6 Gathering User Feedback

Step 1: Observing Operators

Watch how operators interact with the system:

1. Note any confusion or difficulty using the GUI.

2. Identify repetitive tasks that could be automated.

Step 2: Conducting Surveys

Ask operators for their opinions on:

1. Ease of use for the interface.

2. Clarity of notifications and alerts.

3. Perceived accuracy of defect detection.

19.7 Iterating on the System

Step 1: Analyzing Test Data

Use logs and feedback to identify specific areas for improvement:

1. Focus on defects commonly missed by the system.

2. Evaluate inspection times and identify bottlenecks.

Step 2: Implementing Changes

Address high-priority issues first:

- Adjust the AI model for better defect differentiation.

- Streamline the GUI to reduce unnecessary clicks or steps.

Step 3: Retesting

Run another round of field tests after implementing changes to confirm improvements.

19.8 Long-Term Monitoring and Optimization

Continuous Improvement

1. **Regular Updates:** Periodically update the AI model with new training data from real-world operations.

2. **Performance Monitoring:** Use automated tools to track system metrics over time.

Preparing for Scaling

1. Increase camera coverage for larger parts or higher production volumes.

2. Integrate IoT capabilities for remote monitoring and control.

Conclusion

Field testing and optimization are critical steps in ensuring that the Multiview AI Part Inspection System operates reliably and effectively in real-world settings. By systematically evaluating and refining the system, you build a robust tool that meets industrial demands while remaining user-friendly and adaptable. With a focus on continuous improvement, your system will not only achieve but exceed expectations.

Chapter 20: Final Thoughts and Future Improvements

Introduction

Building the Multiview AI Part Inspection System with Raspberry Pi has been an incredible journey of innovation, creativity, and problem-solving. From setting up the foundational hardware and software to implementing advanced features such as real-time defect detection, weekly auto-retraining, and multilingual support, this book has taken you through every step to create a powerful, intelligent inspection system.

In this concluding chapter, we will reflect on the key milestones of the project, summarize its impact, and explore potential directions for future improvements. As technology evolves, there are countless ways to enhance and expand the system to meet emerging demands, ensuring its relevance and effectiveness in the ever-changing landscape of manufacturing and quality control.

20.1 Reflecting on Achievements

Building Blocks of Success

Creating the Multiview AI Part Inspection System required careful planning and meticulous execution. Some of the most impactful milestones include:

1. **Hardware Integration:** Bringing together Raspberry Pi boards, high-resolution cameras, GPIO peripherals, and a touchscreen interface to create a cohesive system.

2. **Software Development:** Developing a robust Python-based framework for image processing, AI classification, and user interaction.

3. **AI Model Training:** Training and deploying a convolutional neural network capable of distinguishing between good parts and various defect types with high accuracy.

4. **User Experience:** Designing a multilingual GUI and integrating feedback mechanisms such as lights, speakers, and notifications for seamless operator interaction.

These components collectively transformed the project from a concept into a tangible, functional system ready for deployment in real-world environments.

System Impact

The inspection system addresses several critical challenges in modern manufacturing:

*   **Efficiency:** Automates part inspection, drastically reducing manual labor and inspection time.

*   **Accuracy:** Leverages AI to improve defect detection rates and minimize human error.

*   **Scalability:** Offers an affordable and adaptable solution for businesses of all sizes, from small workshops to large-scale factories.

20.2 Lessons Learned

Challenges Overcome

Throughout the development process, several challenges required creative solutions:

1. **Hardware Constraints:** Overcoming Raspberry Pi's limited processing power by using lightweight libraries and optimizing performance.

2. **Data Diversity:** Ensuring the AI model performed well across various defect types by expanding and augmenting the training dataset.

3. **Real-Time Processing:** Achieving real-time detection with synchronized multi-camera input by implementing efficient multithreading techniques.

Key Takeaways

- **Modularity Is Key:** Building a system with modular components (hardware, software, and AI) ensures flexibility and easier upgrades.

- **User-Centric Design Matters:** Prioritizing the operator experience through intuitive controls and multilingual support enhances usability and adoption.

- **Data Is Foundational:** Regularly updating the dataset and retraining the model are critical for maintaining system accuracy and relevance.

20.3 Exploring Future Improvements

While the system is fully functional, there are numerous opportunities for refinement and enhancement. Future improvements could focus on expanding capabilities, increasing robustness, and integrating emerging technologies.

Hardware Enhancements

1. **Higher-Resolution Cameras:** Incorporate 4K or higher-resolution cameras to capture even finer details, enabling detection of micro-defects.

2. **Depth Cameras:** Add depth-sensing cameras for 3D imaging, allowing the system to analyze part geometry more comprehensively.

3. **Robotic Integration:** Combine the inspection system with robotic arms for automated part handling, reducing manual input.

Software and AI Advancements

1. **Anomaly Detection Models:** Train unsupervised models capable of detecting unknown defects without relying solely on pre-labeled data.

2. **Edge AI Integration:** Deploy models on hardware accelerators like Google Coral or NVIDIA Jetson for faster inference and reduced latency.

3. **Predictive Analytics:** Use logged inspection data to identify trends and predict potential production issues before they occur.

User Experience

1. **Voice Commands:** Add voice recognition capabilities to the GUI for hands-free operation.

2. **Mobile Integration:** Develop a mobile app that mirrors the system's interface, allowing remote control and monitoring.

3. **Advanced Notifications:** Implement smart notifications that combine defect analysis with actionable insights, such as recommended machine adjustments.

Connectivity and IoT

1. **Cloud Integration:** Expand cloud functionality to include real-time data visualization and remote model updates.

2. **Factory Automation Systems:** Interface with MES (Manufacturing Execution Systems) to streamline workflows and integrate quality control into broader production processes.

20.4 Applications in Emerging Industries

The inspection system, while initially designed for manufacturing, has potential applications across a variety of industries:

1. **Electronics:** Inspecting PCBs (Printed Circuit Boards) and microchips for soldering defects or alignment issues.

2. **Healthcare:** Analyzing medical devices, implants, or pharmaceuticals for quality assurance.

3. **Automotive:** Inspecting engine components, safety-critical parts, or paint finishes for defects.

4. **Aerospace:** Ensuring the integrity of materials and components used in aircraft and spacecraft manufacturing.

Each application may require customization, such as specialized cameras, sensors, or AI models tailored to the unique requirements of the industry.

20.5 Preparing for Scalability

Designing for Growth

As the system is deployed in larger-scale operations, certain considerations will become essential:

1. **Distributed Systems:** Deploy multiple inspection units across different production lines, interconnected through a centralized control system.

2. **Custom AI Models:** Develop specialized models for different product lines, ensuring high accuracy for diverse use cases.

3. **Hardware Redundancy:** Incorporate failover mechanisms to maintain uptime in case of hardware failure.

Training and Support

1. **Documentation:** Create detailed user manuals and troubleshooting guides for operators and technicians.

2. **Training Programs:** Develop training sessions or video tutorials to ensure users are comfortable with the system.

3. **Support Channels:** Establish support channels for quick resolution of technical issues.

20.6 Ethical Considerations and Sustainability

Ethical AI

As the system becomes more autonomous, it's important to ensure transparency and fairness in AI decision-making:

1. **Bias-Free Models:** Regularly audit the AI model to ensure it performs equitably across all part types and defect categories.

2. **Explainability:** Provide clear, interpretable explanations for AI classifications to build trust with users.

Sustainability

1. **Energy Efficiency:** Optimize hardware and software to minimize energy consumption, particularly for large-scale deployments.

2. **Recyclable Components:** Use eco-friendly materials for enclosures and hardware components.

3. **Long-Term Updates:** Ensure the system is designed for longevity, with regular software updates to reduce hardware waste.

20.7 A Vision for the Future

Imagine a future where inspection systems like this are ubiquitous, enabling unparalleled levels of quality assurance and production efficiency. With advancements in AI, robotics, and IoT, the Multiview AI Part Inspection System could evolve into a fully automated solution, capable of predicting and preventing defects before they occur.

This vision is not just about technology—it's about creating smarter, safer, and more sustainable manufacturing processes that benefit businesses, workers, and consumers alike.

Conclusion

The Multiview AI Part Inspection System represents a convergence of innovation and practicality, combining the power of Raspberry Pi, AI, and user-centric design to address real-world challenges. This book has provided you with the knowledge and tools to build and optimize this system, but the journey doesn't end here. Technology continues to evolve, presenting endless opportunities for improvement and adaptation.

As you deploy and expand the system, remember that every iteration brings you closer to perfection. By staying curious, adaptable, and committed to excellence, you can ensure that your inspection system remains at the forefront of quality control technology.

Here's to a future filled with innovation and success!

Sample Python Codes

 # Raspberry Pi AI Inspection System

 # Full system with GUI, camera control, AI inference, GPIO control, TTS, and auto-training

```
import cv2

import os

import time

import threading

import torch

import numpy as np

from gpiozero import LED, Button

from PIL import Image, ImageDraw, ImageTk, ImageFont

from gtts import gTTS

from playsound import playsound

from datetime import datetime

import tkinter as tk

from tkinter import messagebox, filedialog, simpledialog

import glob

import shutil

import locale


# -------------------- CONFIGURATION -------------------- #
```

```python
CAMERA_IDS = [0, 1, 2, 3]  # Camera device IDs

MODEL_PATH = "model.pt"  # Trained model file

DATA_DIR = "data"

LANGUAGES = {"English": "en", "Vietnamese": "vi"}

AUTO_TRAIN_DAY = "Sunday"

LED_GREEN = LED(17)

LED_RED = LED(27)

BUTTON_START = Button(22)

BUTTON_RESET = Button(23)

SPEAKER_LANG = "en"


# -------------------- INITIAL SETUP -------------------- #

part_count = 0

defect_detected = False

selected_language = "English"

defect_labels = ["scratch", "dent", "crack"]  # can be extended
dynamically

preview_paused = False

preview_frames = [None] * 4


# Load model

model = torch.load(MODEL_PATH, map_location=torch.device('cpu'))

model.eval()
```

```python
def speak(text):
    tts = gTTS(text=text, lang=LANGUAGES[selected_language])
    tts.save("temp.mp3")
    playsound("temp.mp3")
    os.remove("temp.mp3")


def capture_images():
    images = []
    for cam_id in CAMERA_IDS:
        cap = cv2.VideoCapture(cam_id)
        ret, frame = cap.read()
        if ret:
            images.append(frame)
        cap.release()
    return images


def classify_images(images):
    global defect_detected
    for i, img in enumerate(images):
        resized = cv2.resize(img, (224, 224))
        input_tensor = torch.tensor(resized).permute(2, 0,
1).unsqueeze(0).float() / 255.0
```

```
    output = model(input_tensor)

    pred = torch.argmax(output, dim=1).item()

    if pred != 0:

        defect_detected = True

        return pred, img  # return defect class and image

    return 0, None


def circle_defect(img):

    h, w, _ = img.shape

    draw = ImageDraw.Draw(Image.fromarray(img))

    draw.ellipse([(w//2-30, h//2-30), (w//2+30, h//2+30)], outline="red",
width=5)

    return img


def reset_counter():

    global part_count

    part_count = 0

    update_gui()


def update_gui():

    count_label.config(text=f"Parts Passed: {part_count}")

    lang_label.config(text=f"Language: {selected_language}")
```

```python
def start_inspection():
    global part_count, defect_detected
    defect_detected = False
    images = capture_images()
    defect_class, defect_image = classify_images(images)

    if defect_detected:
        LED_RED.on()
        LED_GREEN.off()
        speak(f"Defect detected: {defect_labels[defect_class]}")
        # Save and show image
        timestamp = datetime.now().strftime("%Y%m%d_%H%M%S")
        filename = f"defect_{timestamp}.jpg"
        path = os.path.join(DATA_DIR, "defects", filename)
        cv2.imwrite(path, defect_image)
        defect_img = cv2.circle(defect_image, (112, 112), 30, (0, 0, 255), 4)
        cv2.imshow("Defect Detected", defect_img)
        cv2.waitKey(1000)
        cv2.destroyAllWindows()
    else:
        LED_GREEN.on()
        LED_RED.off()
        part_count += 1
```

```python
    speak("One good part")
    update_gui()


def switch_language():
    global selected_language
    keys = list(LANGUAGES.keys())
    i = keys.index(selected_language)
    selected_language = keys[(i + 1) % len(keys)]
    speak(f"Language set to {selected_language}")
    update_gui()


def auto_train():
    today = datetime.today().strftime('%A')
    if today == AUTO_TRAIN_DAY:
        speak("Retraining model with new data")
        # Dummy retrain placeholder (could call script to retrain model)
        time.sleep(2)
        speak("Retraining complete")


def capture_for_labeling():
    timestamp = datetime.now().strftime("%Y%m%d_%H%M%S")
    label_dir = os.path.join(DATA_DIR, "manual_label")
    os.makedirs(label_dir, exist_ok=True)
```
161

```python
    for i, frame in enumerate(preview_frames):
        if frame is not None:
            path = os.path.join(label_dir, f"cam{i}_{timestamp}.jpg")
            cv2.imwrite(path, frame)
    speak("Frames captured for labeling")


def toggle_preview():
    global preview_paused
    preview_paused = not preview_paused
    status = "paused" if preview_paused else "resumed"
    speak(f"Preview {status}")


def add_defect_type():
    global defect_labels
    new_defect = simpledialog.askstring("Add Defect Type", "Enter new defect name:")
    if new_defect:
        if new_defect not in defect_labels:
            defect_labels.append(new_defect)
            speak(f"New defect type {new_defect} added")
        else:
            messagebox.showinfo("Info", "Defect type already exists.")
```

```python
# ------------------- GUI ------------------- #
root = tk.Tk()
root.title("AI Inspection System")
root.geometry("800x480")
root.attributes("-fullscreen", True)


top_frame = tk.Frame(root)
top_frame.pack(pady=10)
count_label = tk.Label(top_frame, text="Parts Passed: 0", font=("Arial", 24))
count_label.pack()
lang_label = tk.Label(top_frame, text="Language: English", font=("Arial", 16))
lang_label.pack()


btn_frame = tk.Frame(root)
btn_frame.pack(pady=30)
tk.Button(btn_frame, text="Start Checking", font=("Arial", 20), width=15, command=start_inspection).pack(pady=5)

tk.Button(btn_frame, text="Reset Counter", font=("Arial", 20), width=15, command=reset_counter).pack(pady=5)

tk.Button(btn_frame, text="Switch Language", font=("Arial", 20), width=15, command=switch_language).pack(pady=5)

tk.Button(btn_frame, text="Capture Frames", font=("Arial", 20), width=15, command=capture_for_labeling).pack(pady=5)
```

```python
tk.Button(btn_frame, text="Pause Preview", font=("Arial", 20),
width=15, command=toggle_preview).pack(pady=5)

tk.Button(btn_frame, text="Add Defect Type", font=("Arial", 20),
width=15, command=add_defect_type).pack(pady=5)


preview_frame = tk.Frame(root)

preview_frame.pack()

preview_labels = []

for i in range(4):

    label = tk.Label(preview_frame)

    label.grid(row=0, column=i, padx=5)

    preview_labels.append(label)


def show_camera_previews():

    global preview_frames

    font = cv2.FONT_HERSHEY_SIMPLEX

    while True:

        if preview_paused:

            time.sleep(0.2)

            continue

        for i, cam_id in enumerate(CAMERA_IDS):

            cap = cv2.VideoCapture(cam_id)

            ret, frame = cap.read()
```

```python
        if ret:
            timestamp = datetime.now().strftime("%H:%M:%S")
            cv2.putText(frame, f"Cam {i} - {timestamp}", (5, 20), font, 0.5,
(255, 255, 255), 1)
            frame = cv2.resize(frame, (200, 150))
            preview_frames[i] = frame.copy()
            img = cv2.cvtColor(frame, cv2.COLOR_BGR2RGB)
            img = Image.fromarray(img)
            imgtk = ImageTk.PhotoImage(image=img)
            preview_labels[i].imgtk = imgtk
            preview_labels[i].configure(image=imgtk)
        cap.release()
    time.sleep(0.2)


def run_gui():
    update_gui()
    auto_train()
    threading.Thread(target=show_camera_previews,
daemon=True).start()
    root.mainloop()


# -------------------- MAIN -------------------- #
if __name__ == '__main__':
```

```python
if not os.path.exists(os.path.join(DATA_DIR, "defects")):
    os.makedirs(os.path.join(DATA_DIR, "defects"))
threading.Thread(target=run_gui).start()
while True:
    if BUTTON_RESET.is_pressed:
        reset_counter()
    time.sleep(0.1)
```

Folder Structure

```
ai_inspection_system/
├── main.py                    # Main script (contains all logic and GUI)
├── model.pt                   # Trained AI model (PyTorch)
├── data/                      # Folder to store all data
│   ├── defects/               # Automatically saved defect images
│   ├── manual_label/          # Manually captured preview frames
│   ├── training/              # Optional: training dataset if retraining locally
│   │   ├── good/              # Good part images
│   │   └── defect_type_1/     # Categorized defect images
│   │   └── defect_type_2/     # ...
├── sounds/                    # Temporary folder for generated voice messages
│   └── temp.mp3               # TTS output before playing
├── assets/                    # Optional: UI icons, background images, etc.
├── utils/                     # Optional: helper scripts (e.g., model training, defect label
│   └── train_model.py         # Sample script to retrain model
├── requirements.txt           # Python dependencies
└── README.md                  # Project documentation
```

www.ingramcontent.com/pod-product-compliance
Lightning Source LLC
LaVergne TN
LVHW052059060326
832903LV00061B/3624